SELF-CARE for FAMILY CAREGIVERS

How to Be More Resilient for Bouncing Back

SELF-CARE FOR FAMILY CAREGIVERS

How to Be More Resilient for Bouncing Back

ELLIE NAZEMOFF
Healthy Lifestyle Advocate, M.S., PhD

Based on the Latest Scientific Research
Educational, Practical, and Resourceful

EN Press

Self-Care for Family Caregivers:

How to Be More Resilient for Bouncing Back

This book is available at a discount when purchased in quantity for sales promotions or corporate use. Special editions, which include personalized covers, excerpts, and corporate imprints can be created when purchased in large quantities. For more information, please email ask@myserenity.love or visit www.myserenity.love

First Edition
ISBN- 978-0-578-37448-2

I dedicate this book to you, the reader, as you ignite the spark within to connect with all that matters. Continue life as a family caregiver, providing compassion and embracing moments that guide you to experience the energy exchange with those you love.

To my children, Valeh and Kaveh, my unconditional loved ones who gave me the greatest joy as a proud mother.
I know you two have a kind heart, which makes me happy, but I also worry, since I know someday you may have to take care of me. As a loving mother, I do not want you to feel obligated, but I guess that is life.
What I wish, is for you to care of yourself FIRST, emotionally and physically. Then I am sure I will be in better care.

Serenity is Contagious

Contents

Life is a balance
of holding on and
letting go.
– Rumi

CHAPTER 1 – INTRODUCTION TO FAMILY CAREGIVING

TEN YEARS AGO, when I was successfully climbing my ladder of success in my technology business, lack of sleep caused high stress that in turn weakened my immune system, and I got seriously sick. To keep my business running when I had a chronic illness was so challenging. But when my father was diagnosed with Alzheimer's, that was a nightmare. Taking care of him certainly was not on my to do list!

I was unfamiliar with the phrase "family caregiver," but naturally that was my new job. I always wanted to make sure my parents were safe and happy in their golden years.

Then I learned how incredibly hard caregiving is. Caring for my parents turned my world upside down. Primarily because of a lack of support. I got so sick that I had no choice but to learn how to stay healthy if I would want to take care of them right.

I took online classes about different kinds of diseases and how to manage stress in tough situations. Well, that helped me a lot, and I wish I had this information ten years ago.

I gathered all the information that helped me during the time that I was taking care of my parents while I was a single mother and running a very complex business. Then of course I had my own health issue. These simple practices helped me to make this family caregiving journey much smoother than it was at the beginning.

The most important part of this journey is to learn how to keep your mind calm and manage your stress. So, this led me to write more about this matter in this book in detail.

When I was thirty-two, I was diagnosed with chronic rheumatoid arthritis (RA). I had no idea why!

Finally, after a couple of months in pain, I was referred to an RA specialist; the doctor asked me if there were any issues in my family or my work. I told him no, and I am happy with my life. He suggested that I should take off from my work and family obligations and stay home for one week, alone, no husband and no children and do nothing, just eat sandwiches, watch fun movies, and think about nothing!

First, I thought he must be crazy. But I had no choice to follow his order. After one week, there was no sign of RA. NOTHING! No pain, no inflammation. I was so happy and back to my life!

Well, Not Really!

You see, I was an immigrant. A single mother of two. A successful business owner. And now, a family caregiver.

My wonderful parents came to the U.S. without knowing English, so their comfort living style is depending on me giving care through various activities. These activities include going to the doctors and filling out forms and translating. Other activities include grocery shopping, being their designated driver, hosting gatherings for their friends, and more. I even took them traveling wherever I would go, and I had no problem doing it. It became a normal way of life for me, until it wasn't.

Seven years later, the RA came back, this time in my right elbow, and I completely forgot about my previous prescription. I was getting Cortisone shots every month for four months until my doctor stopped it and told me to take two weeks' vacation. I told him I couldn't do it. Yet, the doctor said that was the only option I had at that time. I took the vacation, and all was well again. I was back to my life normal life again.

So, I Thought!

Six years later, I was diagnosed with diabetes. I had no clue what diabetes was. It was a fast and progressive condition and seemed to get out of control. It made me so angry because I could not do anything about it.

More insulin to take meant more weight gain. Additionally, I now had sleeping issues. My life was going upside down...at that time, nothing mattered but my children's health and I can how talk about a healthy lifestyle, when I could not even improve mine!

Well, I Did It!

Yes, I got my healthy life back. I stabilized my diabetes under control and understood my body more. I lost all unwanted weight and much more. I lived in a better healthy way, emotionally and physically. I decided to share my findings with my children, and all family caregivers who want to calm their stress (our first enemy).

I'm providing the basic essential insights of good nutrients, a healthy and happier lifestyle. I wish I knew these myself when I was younger.

This book is a science-backed way for all of us to become a little more resilient, so we'll be prepared for whatever life throws at us. I hope this book can be useful to all family caregivers who want to figure out how to be bounce back as they stay healthy while coping with unfamiliar situations.

Additionally, I would like to pass on this information to my children who may take care of me someday so they know that first they must take care of themselves.

This is a new journey for all. Let's enjoy it.

The more you
self-care, the
stronger you
can be.

CHAPTER 2 – WHAT IS FAMILY CAREGIVING?

THERE ARE DIFFERENT TYPES OF CAREGIVERS, but the most common is the family caregiver: any family member, partner, or friend who, regularly and without pay, provides support or care to an elderly person or someone who needs attention around the clock because of a significant or persistent health problem or loss of autonomy.

Often this role is taken on as a natural part of being family to the one being cared for, and most family caregivers do not consider themselves as such.

As medical treatments advance, numbers of people are living with increased chronic illness and disabilities. Thus, more of us find ourselves caring for a loved one at home. Whether you are taking care of an aging parent or a handicapped spouse or a child with a physical or mental illness, providing care for a family member in need is an act of love, kindness, and loyalty. Day after day, you give your care and time to a loved one with your intention to improve their quality of life, without any expectation or gratitude.

Regardless of your circumstances, being a family caregiver is a challenging role and likely one that you haven't been trained to undertake. And like many family caregivers, you probably never anticipated the situation. However, you don't have to be a nursing expert, a superhero, or a saint to be a good family caregiver. With the right help and support, you can be an effective, loving caregiver without having to sacrifice yourself in the process. And that can make family caregiving a more rewarding experience—for both you and your loved one.

Statistics About Family Caregiving

I did not know that more than one in ten Americans act as an unpaid caregiver for an older friend or relative. Over the past three decades, thousands of studies have determined that this significant population is at risk of emotional and physical health consequences.

Did you know that:

· Almost 18% of family caregivers report experiencing fourteen or more days of poor physical health each month.

· More than half of the caregivers say a decline in their health affects their ability to provide care.

· Dementia caregivers report more strain, health problems, and caregiver burnout than non-dementia caregivers.

· 44% are concerned about the emotional strains.

Seven Actions to Create the Self-Care Habit

Some simple actions in my life brought me a happier and healthier life, and throughout this book, I will share them with you. They are simple things like, staying hydrated is one of the best ways to fight off a cold, so you need to make sure your body takes on a lot of fluids. I wish I have learned these sooner, but late is better than never!

Additionally, I trigger your thought with questions, like, is there more to life than work? How can you make sure you are getting a healthy dose of "me time"? I like this phrase.

Focusing on work is a great excuse for not taking care of yourself. I have set specific time where I won't work and will instead spend time with me. First thing in the morning (for example, my meditation time, before 8:00 a.m.) I will explain more about meditation and affirmation in later chapters.

Caring for a sick or aging parent, spouse, or other relative or friend is a true labor of love for many people, but it can also be a significant source of stress. If you regularly provide care for a loved one, you may find yourself feeling stressed, depressed, angry, resentful, guilty, or overwhelmed. These emotions are normal, but they're also a sign that caregivers need to attend to their own needs. If you're one of the nearly 25% of Americans currently providing at least basic assistance for a loved one, consider the following seven steps and do not forget to make your self-care a habit. It has worked for me and others, and I do not doubt that it will work for you as well.

1. **Be honest with your feelings.** If you feel overwhelmed, then you may think that you are suffering from depression. Talk to your health professional if you're feeling stressed or down. It's also a good idea for all caregivers to share their emotions. Here are some options: share with a therapist or share by writing in a daily journal (you can use the weekly journal that I have provided in the bonus chapter of this book.) If you attend a support group, find one that leaves you feeling connected and recharged, rather than discouraged. You can join community groups to support other members.

2. **Be sociable.** Spend quality time with other loved ones, friends, and family at least once a day either away from home or while caregiving, also video chatting helps as well — when time permits.

3. **Ask for help.** You can NOT do everything yourself. Make a list of items that you need assistance with, such as grocery, cleaning, laundry or

watering your plants and say thank you and accept the help when the offer arrives.

4. Day-care or in home care. Adult day-care or in-home care can be a break for caregivers. To locate these and related services, contact your local area agency on aging or eldercare organization (visit www.eldercare.gov to find yours.) There are many other organizations that are near to you that may offer day-care. Ask your library, search the internet, or even ask a health care provider. Once you know more about your loved one's needs, you can draw up a plan for their care. This can include a list of the tasks that you can do as well as those that may need to be farmed out to adult day-care, home health aides, and other resources. If you are your loved one's primary caregiver, you should also discuss finances and legal documents (such as wills and end-of-life requests) with them. Contact your loved one's insurance provider; he or she may be eligible for nutrition services, tax relief, or other benefits.

5. Educate yourself. By educating yourself about your loved one's condition, you'll be better equipped to cope with it. Talk to physicians, visit your local library, and contact related health organizations. If you surf the internet for information, try to avoid personal horror stories or depressing predictions that have been posted by someone with an agenda.

6. Safety-proof your home. Check your home and eliminate potential dangers, such as fire hazards, sharp objects, loose rugs, and cluttered pathways. I am so pleased that I asked a handy man to install horizontal and vertical grab bars inside and outside of my shower for my mother's safety. I am now not as concerned or anxious for a potential fall to occur.

7. Hire help. If being your loved one's sole source of support is too overwhelming, consider hiring a care manager. This professional can help assess your needs and coordinate services. Visit www.caremanager.org for more information.

You are a priority if you want to do your job well.

A good, healthy lifestyle is not just the absence of disease or illness but a state of complete physical, mental, and social well-being. Eating the right nutrition, exercise, resting well, and stress management are important for a healthy lifestyle. But being connected to family and/or friends is a powerful aspect of a healthy life. Smile and laugh out loud several times a day. It keeps you grounded and helps you cope with situations that would otherwise make you crazy.

The most important thing to remember is that you can make a difference in your health and well-being. Take charge of your life and be mindful of small behavior changes that can make your lifestyle a healthier one.

What I know for a fact, this situation, family caregiving, could eat your life if you let it, but remember your life matters too, so balance it out.

You are not alone. But do you feel lonely?

More than 43 million men and women in the U.S. are unpaid caregivers. But whether you care for a child, spouse, parent, or another relative, it's common to feel alone. Feeling alone is an issue that most caregivers will face to some degree during their journey as a caregiver. However, caregivers need not feel ashamed in their journey to find more support.

Whatever the reason, loneliness and caregiving often go hand in hand. As your loved ones needs demand more of your time, you begin to see less and less of friends and family. Until one day, you realize that your social life has faded along with your care recipient's health.

One such study conducted by University of Chicago psychologist, Dr. John Cacioppo, analyzed survey responses from over 2,100 adults ages 55 and over to examine the connections between satisfying relationships and rates of physical and mental decline. He and his team concluded that lacking close personal connections raises an individual's risk of premature death by 14%.

The problem is that, in addition to exacting an extreme emotional toll, loneliness can carry dangerous—even deadly—physical consequences.

Just as low blood sugar triggers a hunger response and pain alert us to potential tissue damage, loneliness also serves as an unconscious warning. Compelling us to satisfy our "hunger" for human connection.

Dr. Cacioppo and his team suggested two following tips for your emotional and physical health: 1. Reach out and ask for what you need. 2. Join a support group.

Again, a healthy lifestyle is a state of complete physical, mental, and social well-being. Eating the right nutrition, exercise, rest well and stress management are important for a healthy lifestyle as well. In the following chapters, you will review health problems that could impact family caregivers because of a lack of a healthy lifestyle, and I believe a healthy lifestyle starts with a healthy mind and emotion.

Tips for New Family Caregivers

I learned as much as I could about my parents' illness and their restrictions and how to care for them. The more I learned, the less anxious I felt about my new role. I became more effective too.

The following helpful tips can support you while caring for someone you love in ways that can benefit both of you.

Search for other caregivers. It helps you to know that you're not alone. It's comforting to give and receive support from others who understand exactly what you're going through.

Listen to your gut. Remember, you know your family member or loved one the best. Don't ignore what doctors and specialists tell you, but listen to your gut too, and share with the healthcare specialist.

Help your loved one to stay independent. Caregiving does not mean doing everything for your loved one. Be open to technologies and strategies that allow your family member to remain as independent as possible. Help your loved one call friends, doctors when they are in need. Show them how to search over the internet or how to ask Siri! Get them started on a puzzle or craft.

Set clear time limits. Be realistic about how much of your time and of yourself you can give. Set clear limits, and communicate those limits to doctors, family members, and other people involved and ask for help if you are in need.

What You May Feel About Being a Family Caregiver

Through this educational research, I found out that many of us feel worried, angry, guilty, or even grieving. The following are my findings of these feelings:

• **Anxiety and worry.** You may worry about how you will handle the additional responsibilities of caregiving and what will happen to your family member if something happens to you. You may also fear what will happen in the future as your loved one's illness progresses.

• **Anger or resentment.** You may feel angry toward the person you're caring for, even though you know it's irrational. Or you might be angry at the world in general, or resentful of other friends or family members who don't have your responsibilities. Well, it is natural to feel that way.

• **Guilt.** You may feel guilty for not doing more, being a "better" caregiver, having more patience, accepting your situation with more composure, or, in the case of long-distance caregiving, not being available more often.

• **Grief.** Many losses can come with caregiving (for example, the healthy future you envisioned with your spouse or child; the goals and dreams you've had to set aside). If the person you're caring for is terminally ill, you're also dealing with that grief.

When you understand why you're feeling the way you do; it can still be upsetting. To deal with your feelings, it's important to talk about them. Don't keep your emotions inside of yourself; find at least one person you trust to share your emotions with. Someone who'll listen to you without interruption or judgment.

Communication Do's and Don'ts

Do's . . .

Make Them Feel Safe - Avoid becoming frustrated by empathizing and remembering that your loved one can't help their condition. Making them feel safe rather than stressed will make communication easier. Take a short break if you feel your fuse getting short. My mother, who was so strong all her life, now needs help for putting her clothes on. I was thinking that she was becoming lazy until I learned about her condition. Then, I understood her better, with less frustration for me.

Make It Simple - Keep communication simple, short, and clear. Give one direction or ask one question at a time. Understanding my father's condition, Alzheimer's, I learned that one task at a time is much easier for him and me. When I asked him to get ready, I used to say, "We are going out. Put your sweater, shoes, and hat on." My father just looked at me. What was I thinking? Then when I asked him, "Dad, put your sweater on please," he did it right away.

Tell your loved one who you are if there appears to be any doubt. Call your loved one by name. My children and I call my mother Maman Mary, and my father Baba Nazi. That way they know that we are close to them.

Speak Slowly - Your loved one may take longer to process what's being said. Believe me, at the beginning of this journey, I completely lost and kept asking myself, *"why do they do that to me and not responding to my questions?"* Well, I learned that as we age it takes longer to understand and respond. I also learned to ask questions that can be answered with "yes" or "no." For example, ask, "Did you like your breakfast?" instead of "What did you have for breakfast?"

Find a different way to say the same thing if it wasn't understood the first time. Try a simpler statement with fewer words. For example, say "Isn't it cold? Let's put our jackets on." If that doesn't work, go to "Put your jacket on please." Don't talk down to a person with dementia. They will feel angry or hurt.

Fib - If telling the whole truth will upset the person with dementia, use a fibbing technique. For example, to answer the question, "Where is my brother?" it may be better to say, "He is not here right now," instead of "He died 10 years ago."

Repeat Many Times - Be prepared to say the same things over and over as the person can't recall them for more than a few minutes at a time. Additionally, it is better to say it with a smile, eye contact, nice gestures, and hugs.

Involve - Keep your loved one involved. My daughter engages my mother with picture puzzles, which are meditative activities and have long been thought to decrease feelings of anxiety and increase mental well-being. Studies have connected jigsaw puzzles to improved cognition in the elderly.

One thing that I recommend is to ask your loved one to do something for you because everyone loves to be needed. Once, I asked my mother to knit a shawl for me. She enjoys it, plus it frees up my time for "me-time"! Now, everyone in the family has a nice and useable gift from her. Focusing on a knitting project allows seniors to sit down and relax for a few minutes. As seniors knit, the heart rate slows down, and their blood pressure lowers. Over time, reduced anxiety and lower blood pressure provides long-term health benefits such as preventing heart disease. One more benefit to knitting is that it prevents arthritis and tendinitis!

What are some do's you can think of that can potentially benefit your situation? I started with a few varieties of activities to see what works. Do not give up. Try different things, patiently, to see what sticks.

Don'ts...

Don't ever say things like: "Do you remember?" "Try to remember!" "Did you forget?" "How could you not know that?!"

My mother hates this way of talking. And so do I. Don't you?

Ask questions that challenge short-term memory such as "Do you remember what we did last night?" The answer will likely be no, which may be humiliating for the person with dementia. What I do is, I say, "Mom, last night we had a good time at the pier, watching the moon."

Don't ever say "I just told you that." Instead, just repeat it over and over.

Make behavioral directions clear. For example, instead of "sit there," say, "sit in the green chair please."

One of the things that I am grateful for in this new world is access to technology. Use the internet for your research and share your findings with your friends and with us at www.myserenity.love

In the following chapters, you will learn about the health issues, how to prevent and fix them. Included will be topics about stress, anxiety, and depression, which could cause other illnesses by interrupting our mindfulness, sleep, and nutrition. That leads us to a lack of movement and other issues such as inflammation.

CHAPTER 3 – BALANCING YOUR LIFE

YOUR MIND, BODY AND HEALTH are critical components of providing care to your family. It's important for you to keep yourself healthy and balanced. In this book, I have covered a wide range of health topics. Keep your life journey simple and easy so you could enjoy every moment.

Emotional Needs of Family Caregivers

For a long time, I would not take time off to relax, because I had this impression that I was ignoring my parent's needs, and they needed my constant attention. I was wrong, I realized it when I was hospitalized for high blood pressure. "Uh, no, what is happening to them now?" It was my first response soon after my condition stabilized. I then understood that I could support them more when I was feeling better, healthier, and stronger.

7 actionable tips you can take to strengthen your health:

    1. Talk with someone to make sense of your situation and your feelings about it. There's no better way of relieving stress than spending time face-to-face with someone who cares about you.

2. Keep a journal. Some people find it helpful to write down their thoughts and feelings to help them see things more clearly. At the end of this book, a guided journal is provided, use it!

3. Watch out for signs of depression, anxiety, or burnout and seek professional help if needed. It is very important to study and learn how to be resilient and bounce back.

4. Stay social. Make it a priority to visit regularly with other people. Nurture your close relationships. Don't let yourself become isolated.

5. Find a community. Fortunately, I live in a community that offers many different programs and events. One of the best ways to find new friends and get involved in neighborhood activities is to join local clubs and volunteer groups. To find social groups, your local library is a good place to start. Libraries often host events around books and recreational topics. Your local community center will also have resources for finding social groups and clubs. Find like-minded people who understand you. If you do not feel comfortable around others, then ask one of your friends and family members to join you.

6. Do things you enjoy. Do something that you enjoy doing. During the COVID-19 pandemic, I learned how to cook better, and how to garden. These activities made my life more meaningful because I do them with joy. From the time that I pick fresh vegetables or plant some new herbs, cooking and gardening have become part of my daily meditation routine. Try to find meaning in both your life and in your role as a caregiver.

7. Maintain balance in your life. Although I have a new hobby, gardening, that does not mean I quit my job. I love to work in my own company that I established more than thirty years ago. It is part of who I am. But I learned to maintain balance in my life, which was not easy at first. Giving value to being alive and living well, became the answer. Here are 4 examples you can try too:

- **Exercise regularly.** Try to get in at least thirty minutes of exercise, three times per week. Exercise is a great way to relieve stress and boost your energy. So, get moving, even if you're tired. When COVID-19 happened and we had to stay home, three generations, my mother, my daughter, and I, we had no choice but to redecorate my living room to the gym. It is perhaps one of the best decisions we made. Watching TV while we are biking, rowing, doing Pilates and / or yoga. I love swimming and I take my mother with me to the pool. This is our relaxing time, whether it is indoor or outdoor pool. Both of us can have some great time with great movements in different skill levels. Plus, with aqua exercises, my mother is safe in the water, and I can do my exercise movements at the same time we are both in the water.

- **Eat right.** Well-nourished bodies are better prepared to cope with stress and get through busy days. Keep your energy up and your mind clear by eating nutritious meals at regular intervals throughout the day. My other new hobby, thanks to COVID-19, is cooking fresh meals. I am now a decent good chef, and I am loving it! Sometimes good things happen to us in worse situations. I never had real time to cook until now. Since we could not go to restaurants, I had no choice but to learn to cook at home. The more I cooked, the more fun it became, especially from my vegetable garden. When you put your heart to anything, you become capable of doing it. This is the best way to eat right. I've included my healthy recipes in the bonus chapter of this book.

- **Get enough sleep.** Aim for an average of six to eight hours of solid, uninterrupted sleep every night. Otherwise, your energy level, productivity, and ability to handle stress will suffer. I intentionally ignore nonsense news. Instead, I meditate before going to bed.

- **Keep up with your health.** Go to the doctor and dentist on schedule, regularly. Keep up with your prescriptions and/or medical therapy. As a caregiver, you need to stay strong and healthy as much as possible. To set reminders for yourself and your loved one for action items like taking medications, use your cell phone "Reminder" application.

Two Self-Care Formulas

To help you with self-care, I'll share with you two of my formulas. They changed my life. The first formula is about a healthier life, while the second formula is for a happier life. Follow them and set your phone to remind you which steps you should take—one of the smartest tricks your phone can do with the "Reminder" app.

Formula #1 for a Healthier Life

Morning Routine:

• **Meditation / Affirmation** - There are many different types of meditation, but they all come down to one basic tenet: relaxing the mind and trying to focus on the breath. Meditation is a way to exercise the unconscious mind, practice mindfulness, and lessen anxieties.

Research has shown that meditation has many mental and physical health benefits. It can help improve sleep, better focus, concentration, manage pain, lower blood pressure, and fostering kindness.

A good morning starts with an affirmation. Open your mind to positivity with sayings such as, "I am excited to learn something new today!" Say it with enthusiasm and meaning. Examples are in the bonus chapter.

• **Breakfast** - Do you know why a healthy breakfast is important? These are just some of the reasons:

o   Has brain-boosting powers

o   Provides essential nutrients

o   Good for the heart

o   Enhances the immune system

o   Improves skin texture and tone

In the bonus chapter, I provide a healthy and simple breakfast recipe which I call FePi. FePi is a combination of Feta cheese and Pita bread (also referred to as Naan or Lavash bread.) If you desire, you can add one tablespoon of honey. It is that simple and all you need to get going. Of course, it goes well with a cup of coffee or tea.

• **Medications and Supplements** - Many family caregivers forget to take their own medications. I was one of them. Now anytime I give my mother's medication in the morning I take mine as well. Believe me it is easy to forget, unless you make it a habit for yourself and set reminders using "Reminder" app types.

The best time to take many vitamins (not all of them) and minerals is in the morning. They are soluble vitamins that are energy-boosting and stressbusting. Some of the most popular **B vitamins** are **Vitamin B-complex** which focuses on eight B vitamins:

B-1 (thiamine), B-2 (riboflavin), B-3 (niacin), B-5 (pantothenic acid), B-6 (pyridoxine), B-7 (biotin), B-9 (folic acid), B-12 (cobalamin)

Note: For a good start to your day, take B vitamin on an empty stomach when you first wake up in the morning. Your supplements may be recommended or packaged for the morning, noon, or evening dosages, based on individual health needs.

While **vitamin C** is a largely helpful nutrient. It is a water-soluble nutrient, which is best absorbed when you take them on an empty stomach. An ideal way would be to take your supplement first thing in the morning, 30-45 minutes before your meal.

Vitamin D is also inversely related to the sleep hormone melatonin. This makes sense, because, if we are getting your vitamin D naturally with the help from the sun, you are synthesizing it during the day. So, it's usually better to take vitamin D supplements in the morning. That will maximize your absorption of calcium. If you take a supplement that also contains vitamin D, it will help your body absorb calcium more efficiently. The best is to take calcium tablets with a meal about 2 hours before and 4 hours after taking any other supplements that might interfere with your calcium supplement.

NOTE: I have added more information about the benefit of supplements in the nutrition section in this book.

Afternoon / Mid-Day Routine:

• **Lunch** - An important meal for everyone is lunch, because it provides energy and nutrients to keep our body and brain working efficiently into the evening. A homemade lunch can be a healthy and delicious choice and gives you control over the foods and ingredients included. I included a recipe in the bonus chapter for a dish I call TATA. I can make it the night before and have it for lunch the next day.

• **Drink Tea** - According to WebMD, researchers followed more than 37,000 people in the Netherlands for thirteen years in one of the largest and longest studies ever to examine the impact of tea drinking on heart health. They found that people who drank three to six cups of tea per day had a 45% lower risk of death from heart disease than people who drank less than one cup of tea a day. Research shows that the advantages of drinking tea are good for you whether it's white, green, or black. Tea clears your arteries. Tea calms inflammation.

Drinking tea around 3 p.m. is very beneficial to the human body, as it can increase the immune system and prevent flu and colds. No wonder the beautiful British afternoon tea is so special and classy.

• **Take a Walk** - Walking is a great way to improve and maintain your overall health. Just fifteen minutes every day can help your heart, strengthen bones, reduce excess body fat, boost muscle power and endurance. It can also reduce your risk of developing conditions such as type 2 diabetes, osteoporosis, and some cancers. Unlike some other forms of exercise, walking is free and doesn't require any special equipment or training. It also improves self-perception, self-esteem, mood, and sleep quality. It reduces stress, anxiety, and fatigue. When I cannot walk, I swim, or I bike.

Evening Routine:

• **Eat Salad** - Salad green contains vitamin A, C, beta-carotene, calcium, folate, fiber, and phytonutrients. Leafy vegetables are a good choice for a healthful diet because they do not contain cholesterol and are naturally low in calories and sodium.

Salad's other contributors to heart health include the ever-useful antioxidants, like vitamin C in broccoli, strawberries, and bell peppers, vitamin E in sunflower. Eating salad greens in your daily life is one of the healthiest habits you can adopt.

Sometimes we want a hot and fun dinner. I provide a healthy alternative recipe in the bonus chapter for a dish I call ZAZAZA. It is an easy to make flatbread filled with healthy vegetables (onion, mushroom, green pepper, tomato.) You can invite your friends and your loved one to share with. That is what I do since my mother loves pizza.

• **Listen to Music** - Research has shown that blood flows more easily when music is played. It can also reduce heart rate, lower blood pressure, decrease cortisol (stress hormone) levels, and increase serotonin and endorphin levels in the blood. It elevates mood. Music can boost the brain's production of the hormone dopamine.

I like listening to Spanish guitar and soft jazz. Music helps my mother's mood too. When she notices that I am happy and when I am in a good mood it affects her mood. Music has special power to everyone's life.

• **Call a Friend** - True and real friends are hard to come by. If you happen to have one or two great ones, treat them well. If you do not have one, open your heart, say hello with smile to all you like and give a friendship note to them.

Keep in mind that everyone wants a good and positive friend with a sense of humor and someone that adds value to the friendship. Perhaps you should share your findings about healthy vegetable recipes, herbs and even a good movie you like to watch and then discuss about.

People with good friends tend to have stronger immune systems and anti-inflammatory responses that can lead to quicker wound healing and reduce the risk of illnesses, including cardiovascular disease, arthritis, and some cancers.

A friend is someone who knows you well and accepts you as is. I believe my friends are my family that I chose.

The next time you're stressed, take a few minutes to call a friend with a caring ear. Don't text them. Don't email them. Just call them. And be that caring ear for them too.

Bedtime Routine:

• **Journal** – Journaling is a powerful keystone habit you can apply to your daily life. If done correctly, you will show up better in every area of your life. Journaling has been found to reduce worry and stress, increase sleep time, and improve sleep quality. Also, I write my next day agenda (grabbing the mail, make doctor appointments, go to the nail salon, etc.)

Set aside 15 minutes each night for writing about a recent positive experience. Write about not only what happened, but also how you felt at the time. Many mental health experts recommend journaling because it can improve your mood and manage symptoms of depression. It may also make therapy work better.

As a bonus, I have provided a weekly journal for your convenience in the last section of this book.

• **Read a Book** – Reading before you sleep could relax you significantly. A 2009 study from researchers at the University of Sussex showed that six minutes of reading reduces stress by 68% (more relaxing than either music or a cup of tea). Thus, clearing the mind and getting the body ready for sleep.

Reading has been associated with a lot of benefits from a greater sense of empathy to a decreased risk of dementia. Doctors at the Mayo Clinic suggest reading as part of a regular sleep routine.

It's even more effective than drinking tea or taking a relaxing walk. Reading for just six minutes can drastically reduce stress levels.

• **Skincare** – One of my "me time" before bedtime is focusing on my skin's well-being. I first take a shower. Taking a deep breath and enjoying the smell of my rose shower gel. Taking a shower before sleeping is one of the best habits to help you unwind and release muscle tension. It also helps regulate your blood pressure.

After shower, it is good to moisturize your face and body with oils that won't clog your skin pores.

What kind of face oils to use? Here are my helpful face oil tips to add to your skincare regime:

   o   Anti-aging use argan oil. Argan oil is safe to use on oily and/or acne-prone skin. Why? Because argan oil won't clog your pores (it's non-comedogenic), and the oleic and linoleic acids in argan oil help balance the skin.

   o   Acne use tea tree oil.

   o   Oily skin use grapeseed oil.

   o   Skin repairs use black currant oil.

   o   Sensitive skin use chamomile oil.

• **Massage Your Neck** – This is really a good way to relax yourself. In the sitting position, using the fingers of both hands, massage the back of your neck along the line of your skull, starting from the middle out towards the back of your ears. Breathe with every stroke and feel the tension released. Do this with purpose, focusing on each breath.

• **Breathe Deeply** – Breathing exercises can be helpful to reduce stress and anxiety and help you to relax at bedtime.

When you are under excessive anxiety, your brain does not get the oxygen it needs to think properly and have maximum clarity. When you pay attention to your breathing and practice deep breathing exercises, you fully oxygenate your brain, which enhances your ability to think and allows the brain to have optimal clarity. Deep breathing affects abdominal organs, improves the immune system, encourages good posture, improves the function of your nervous system, strengthens your lungs, improves memory, and more.

Here is a breathing technique I use called the 4:7:8 Deep Breathing Routine:

o   Let go of all thoughts and clear your mind

o   Slowly breathe in through your nose (4 seconds)

o   Hold that breath for about 7 seconds

o   Exhale through the mouth at 2x the speed it took to inhale

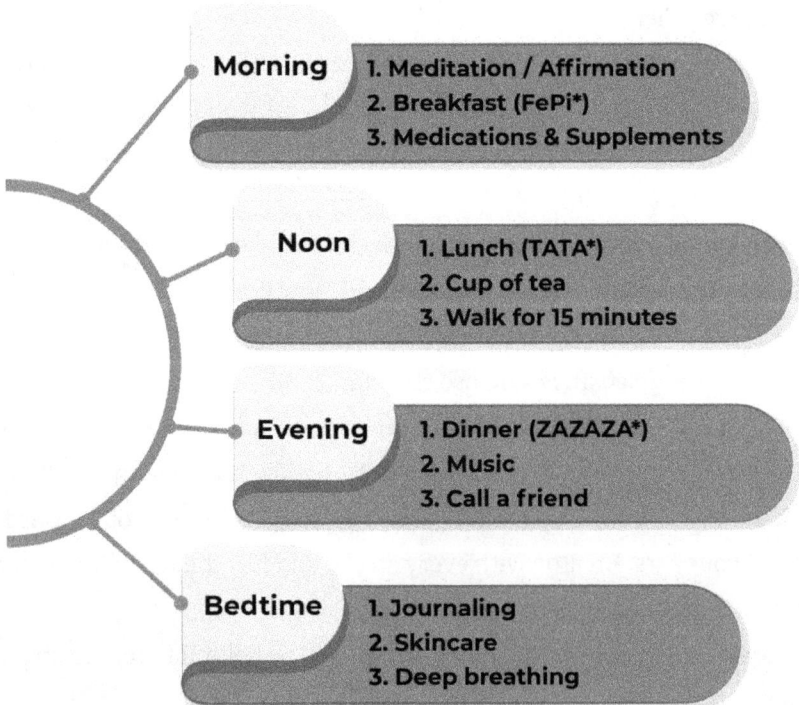

Morning
1. Meditation / Affirmation
2. Breakfast (FePi*)
3. Medications & Supplements

Noon
1. Lunch (TATA*)
2. Cup of tea
3. Walk for 15 minutes

Evening
1. Dinner (ZAZAZA*)
2. Music
3. Call a friend

Bedtime
1. Journaling
2. Skincare
3. Deep breathing

Image 3-1 Infographic of Self-Care Formula for a Healthier Life

Formula #2 for a Happier Life

The second formula is *Self-Care for a Happier Life*. Although a healthy life and a happy life go hand in hand, I showed you a quick way for reminding yourself about what to do for a healthier life, and now an easier way to have a happier life every day. It is meant to be easy and simple for you to enjoy more of your life. This will open your heart for more love, activities, and more laughter.

Being happy is the feeling of truly enjoying your life. Scientific evidence suggests that being happy may have major benefits for your health. For starters, being happy promotes a healthy lifestyle. Being happy can boost your immune system, which might help you fight off the common cold and chest infections and protect your heart and reduce pain. Being happy can help lower blood pressure, which may decrease the risk of heart disease.

Focusing on the things that make you happy will not only improve your life — it may help extend it too. Especially for you as a family caregiver, it is important to focus on yourself, listen to your heart, and make time to relax, which brings you a happier life.

After a long time searching for my own happiness, I found out that you must first be healthy, otherwise, no matter how successful you are in business, and how rich or famous you are, if you are not healthy you cannot be happy. A healthy life and happy life complement each other. You cannot have a healthy life if you are not happy. Same as you cannot be happy if you are not healthy.

4 Easy Steps to a Happier Lifestyle:

• **Meditate in Motion or Movement Meditation** - According to WebMD, Yoga does more than burn calories and tone muscles. It's a total mind-body workout that combines strengthening and stretching poses with deep breathing and meditation or relaxation. There are more than 100 different forms of yoga. Some are fast-paced and intense.

According to Mayo Clinic, Tai-chi is a series of gentle physical exercises and stretches. Each posture flows into the next without pause, ensuring that your body is in constant motion. Tai-chi is sometimes described as meditation in motion because it promotes serenity through gentle movements — connecting the mind and body.

Additionally, caring for your garden can be a great form of mindfulness meditation. By connecting with the earth and with the practice of gardening, you can cultivate a healthy mind and feel calm and connected. Simply planting a seed with intention, or touching soil, can be transformative. Also gardening with your loved one who you are taking care of, could be one of the best ways to spend time together and create good memories. Any time my mom and I are spending time in my backyard, we both feel better and happier. We talk about herbs and flowers, and that communication is very healthy and uplifting for the both of us.

• **Eat a Healthier Diet** - Studies show that the more fruits and vegetables you eat, the happier you will be. Eating fruits and vegetables are all great ways to help improve your mood. Being happy promotes a range of lifestyle habits that are important for the overall health. Happy people tend to eat healthier diets, with higher intakes of fruits, vegetables, and whole grains. A healthy diet helps you be happier and being happy helps you to eat healthy food.

• **Spend Time with Friends Who Uplift You and Make You Smile** - I like this quote very much, "Surround yourself with people who make you happy. People who make you laugh, who help you when you are in need. People who genuinely care. They are the ones worth keeping in your life. Everyone else is just passing through." — Karl Marx

· **Learn Something New** - Do things you love, find purpose, and be generous. Most importantly, learn something new and try new things like playing music. My next things to learn is playing the piano. Playing an instrument can act as a meditation in that it can take you away from the day to day and let you focus on the simple movements. Researchers have found that learning to play a musical instrument can enhance verbal memory, four-dimensional reasoning, and learning skills. Playing an instrument makes you use both sides of your brain, which strengthens memory power. Music can also be a way to express your emotions. When you play an instrument, sad and nervous feelings can diminish, or when you're happy, the music can make you happier.

Follow these two self-care formulas and share with us how you are doing with them on my site, www.myserenity.love

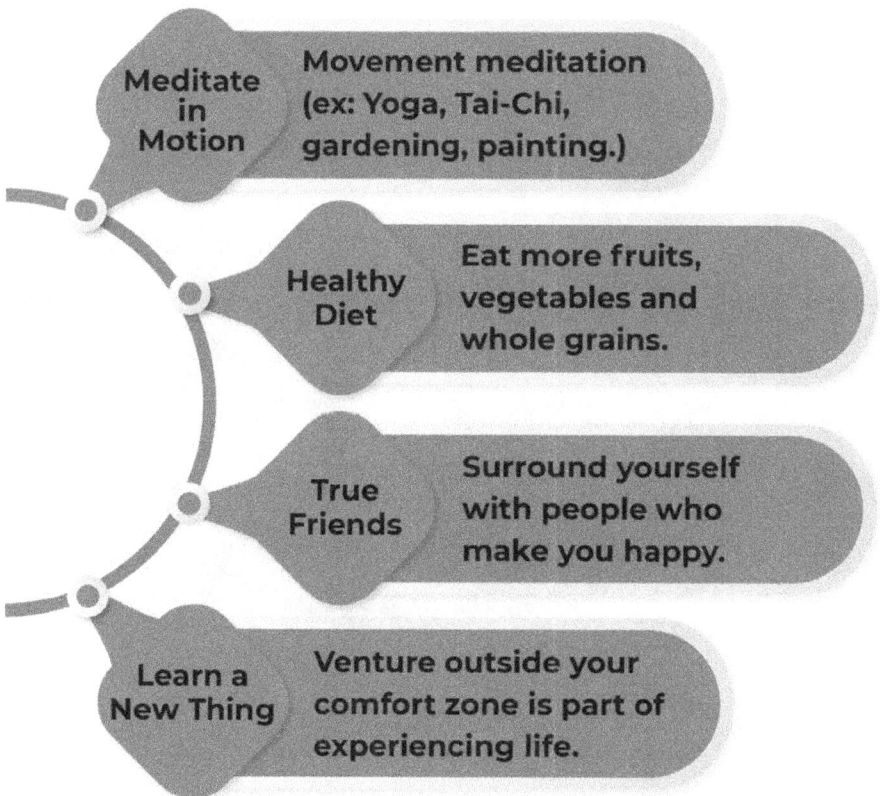

Meditate in Motion — Movement meditation (ex: Yoga, Tai-Chi, gardening, painting.)

Healthy Diet — Eat more fruits, vegetables and whole grains.

True Friends — Surround yourself with people who make you happy.

Learn a New Thing — Venture outside your comfort zone is part of experiencing life.

Image 3-2 Infographic of Self-Care Formula for a Happier Life

Now that you have the formulas for healthier and happier lifestyle, in the following chapters I share with you my journey and latest scientific information I've applied that works.

In Chapter 4, I share about the mental awareness and mindful changes to live a healthier and happier life.

In Chapter 5, I share about the physical body, including easy exercises and activities.

In Chapter 6, I discuss the nutrient benefits

In Chapter 7, I provide insight to preventive measures to consider.

Are you ready? Let's get going on to the next chapter then.

CHAPTER 4 – YOUR MENTAL HEALTH

$\mathbf{W}$E HAVE LEARNED THAT A HEALTHY MIND can help achieve a healthy body. This chapter is about why and how it is important as a caregiver to maintain your mental health.

Did you know that there is a syndrome for family caregivers' stress? WebMD characterizes Caregiver Stress Syndrome as a condition of physical, mental, and emotional exhaustion. It typically results from a person neglecting their own physical and emotional health because they are focused on caring for an ill, injured, or disabled loved one.

According to the Mayo Clinic, as the population ages, more caregiving is being provided by people who aren't health care professionals. About one in three adults in the United States provides care to other adults as informal caregivers. The symptoms of caregiver burnout are much like the symptoms of stress and depression.

A study by the National Alliance for Caregiving (NAC) and the AARP Public Policy Institute found the average age of a family caregiver is 49—where nearly 10% are seniors themselves. Caregivers over the age of seventy-five are most likely taking care of a spouse or partner. Caregivers spend an average of 24.4 hours a week providing care, but 23% spend more than 41 hours per week caregiving. Of course, there are many other situations—for example, let's look at mine. My mom is with me 24 hours a day, but I have learned how to manage my situation.

I read many books and articles regarding family caregiving and how to stay healthy and happy. But I am a human, and I get exhausted too. Yet, the more I learned, the more I relaxed. I found out that I am not the only one with this situation. Perhaps not many people like me want to learn the root of this problem and want to fix it in the right way. To me, stress has a major role in our healthy life. Most caregivers report experiencing stress, depression, and emotional problems at least twice a month, according to the CDC. Shockingly, nearly 15% report experiencing these conditions at least fourteen days a month.

You know, everyone experiences stress and anxiety at one time or another. Stress is a response to a threat in a situation. Anxiety is a stress reaction. Family caregiver stress is due to the emotional and physical strain of caregiving. Family caregivers report much higher levels of stress than people who are not caregivers. Many family caregivers are providing help or are "on-call" almost all day. Sometimes, this means there is little time for work or activities with other family members or friends.

The Impact of Anxiety, Depression, and Stress

An estimated 31.1% of U.S. adults experience anxiety disorder at some time in their lives, according to the National Institute of Mental Health.

Depression is more than just feeling down or having a bad day. When a sad mood lasts for a long time and interferes with normal, everyday functioning, you may be depressed, as defined by CDC.

It is interesting that the exact cause of depression is unknown. It may be caused by a combination of genetic, biological, environmental, and psychological factors. Everyone is different, but going through a major life change, even if it was planned, can cause depression.

Stress is your body's way of responding to any kind of demand. It can be caused by both good and bad experiences.

Stress increases the amount of a hormone in your body called cortisol, which can lead to overeating and cause your body to store fat. Women with higher levels of stress are more likely to have problems getting pregnant than women with lower levels of stress.

Stress suppresses the immune system, which makes it easier for you to get sick. Some of the symptom's stress can lead to are low blood sugar, thyroid problems, heart attacks, cholesterol, etc. Some of the most common symptoms are headaches or abdominal pains, dizzy spells, heavy breathing, insomnia, sweating, sleep disorders, tiredness, fatigue, distraction, impaired sexual performance, and nightmares.

Sometimes stress also appears in the form of phobias or psychological disorders. We need to prevent it, but how? By understanding the cause.

Psychological and emotional signs of stress include:
- Depression or anxiety
- Anger and irritability
- Feeling overwhelmed and unmotivated
- Sleeping problem
- Constant worry
- Problems with your memory or concentration

Popular physical symptoms that can cause stress include:
- Aches and pains
- Diarrhea and constipation
- High blood pressure
- Nausea, dizziness
- Chest pain, rapid heart rate
- Frequent colds or flu

The Difference Between Anxiety, Depression, and Stress

Anxiety, which has no clear cause, tends to last longer and be more difficult to treat than stress. Stress typically goes away when the stressors disappear. However, chronic stress can escalate into anxiety or depression, so it's important to take steps to reduce or eliminate stress whenever possible.

If you're not sure whether you're suffering from stress, anxiety, or depression, don't delay in talking to a health care provider to get the help you need. The journey to recovery begins with defining the cause of your issues and getting the right treatment.

Depression and anxiety are serious but treatable illnesses. The same medications may be used to ease the symptoms of each condition. The two also share similar symptoms, like nervousness, irritability, insomnia, and problems concentrating, but each has its causes.

Anxiety is when you feel stressed long after the actual event has passed. This constant feeling of being stressed, even though the stimulus does not exist anymore is classified as anxiety.

Worry over money, loved ones, friendships, bullies, and job pressures are all examples of ongoing stressed feelings that can be called anxiety. Social anxiety is something that has been observed to be on the rise.

A new study shows that being stressed out for a long period might increase anxiety, The study, published in Behavioral Neuroscience, lays some of the blame on stress hormones. Those stress hormones, such as cortisol and corticotropin-releasing hormone, can help us respond to an immediate threat.

It has been estimated that about 85% of patients with depression also experience significant symptoms of anxiety, according to the NIH.

When you're depressed, it affects just about everything in your life — how you think, feel, behave, and function. You may experience one or more of these symptoms:

- Discouragement
- Sadness
- Hopelessness
- Anger
- Lack of motivation or interest in life in general
- Low energy level
- Insomnia

If these feelings last longer than two weeks and interfere with daily activities like spending time with friends, caring for your family, or going to work, most likely you're experiencing a major depressive episode.

Depression is more than just feeling down. While nearly all of us feel sad, moody, or down from time to time, people who are depressed have these feelings much more intensely and for longer periods, often for weeks, months, and even years. They find it hard to function and do a lot to hide their depression.

Depression is one of the most common mental illnesses we have in society today, and it has been estimated that one in five people will experience it at some stage in their life.

Depression is classified in terms of its severity: mild, moderate, and severe. Here are some physical manifestations of depression that might help you pinpoint the disease, and thus, fight it.

Depression is a chronic disease as well as a common illness; 14% of older adults sought treatment for depression, which is a treatable medical condition that is not a normal part of aging.

Steps you can take to help with depression include:

• **Manage stress levels.** Reach out to family and friends during rough spells and consider regular meditation.

• **Eat a healthy diet.** What you put into your body can affect your mood, so focus on foods that are high in nutrients and promote the release of endorphins and those "feel-good" chemicals, and limit consumption of things like alcohol, caffeine, artificial sweeteners, and highly processed foods.

• **Routine exercise.** Exercise has several physical and psychological benefits, including improving your mood through the release of endorphins and other "feel-good" brain chemicals, boosting self-confidence, and improving your physical appearance. And increased socialization through interactions at gyms and group classes.

• **Talk to your doctor.** If you've experienced any of the warning signs of depression, ask your doctor about treatment options.

Stress is usually a precursor to anxiety, and anxiety is usually a precursor to depression. If you have an anxiety disorder, you may experience fear, panic, and anxiousness. Untreated, these disorders can limit your ability to work, maintain relationships or even leave the house.

The difference between them is that stress is a response to a threat in a situation. Anxiety is a stress reaction. Whether in good times or bad, most people say that stress interferes at least moderately with their lives.

Stress and anxiety are not always bad. In the short term, they can help you overcome a challenge or dangerous situation. Examples of everyday stress and anxiety include worrying about finding a job, feeling nervous before a big test, or being embarrassed in certain social situations.

Stress and anxiety are common experiences for most people. Stress management is necessary for everyone in modern life. To monitor your stress, first identify your triggers: what makes you feel angry, tense, worried, or irritable? Do you often get headaches or an upset stomach with no medical cause?

Examples of life stresses could be:

- Every year you are getting older and rounder
- You do not find time to exercise
- Lack of discipline to eat healthy
- Chronic illness
- Getting married or getting a divorce
- Moving to a new house

Activities to Manage Stress and Anxiety

According to many resources such as Healthline.com, activities such as walking or jogging that involve repetitive movements of large muscle groups can be particularly stress relieving.

Regular exercise can help lower stress and anxiety by releasing endorphins and improving your sleep and self-image.

Following are what CDC recommends in coping with stress:

- Take deep breaths, stretch, or meditate
- Eating healthy, well-balanced meals
- Exercise regularly
- Get plenty of sleep
- Avoid excessive alcohol, tobacco, and substance use
- Continue with routine preventive measures (such as vaccinations, cancer screenings, etc.)

WebMD suggests talking to your doctor if you feel down or anxious for more than several weeks. In the meantime, there are things you can learn to manage stress. Physical activity can help improve your sleep. Foods like beans, fruits, berries, vegetables, and spices such as ginger can also be very helpful.

The saying goes that laughter is the best medicine, and there's truth to that. Laughter releases dopamine and other feel-good chemicals in the brain, all of which can help decrease stress.

According to Dr. Weil, for some years, research has suggested that laughter really is healing. It may boost immunity, relieve pain, lower stress, and even help protect against heart disease.

One of the latest studies, from Loma Linda University in California, found that humor may help reduce damage to the brain caused by the stress hormone cortisol, which in turn, can improve memory, thus lowering stress (through laughter, in this case).

Twenty minutes of laughter a day may not keep the doctor away, but it may help keep your immune system working properly.

I found a very interesting article on the AARP site "How to Strengthen Your Lungs to Fight COVID-19", that got my attention about how right breathing can help us in many ways, physically and mentally.

In that article, Bruce Levy, Chief of the Division of Pulmonary and Critical Care Medicine at Brigham and Women's Hospital in Boston, suggested this technique; "Slowly take in a big, deep breath through your nose, allowing your belly to rise as you fill your lungs, and hold it there for a few seconds. Exhale fully. Repeat a few times, and then force yourself to cough, so you bring up any secretions. (Make sure you wear a mask if there are people nearby.)"

I believe that meditation is not only about sitting, closing your eyes, and breathing deeply. Anytime you calm your brain, distract yourself from anything that bothers your nervous system, which causes your body to release stress hormones like cortisol and adrenaline, can be a form of meditation.

Here are some sample activities that can help you relax:
• **Gardening**. Gardening is another form of meditation that can restore the body and soul. Gardening has many other benefits like absorbing vitamin D from the sun when you are growing your own vegetable and flowers. You reap

what you sow. In the case of a vegetable garden, a rich harvest may bring more than dinner.

Gardening is good for your body and mind. It can also help reduce stress and anxiety levels and offer light physical activity.

But are you wondering what to grow? Consider a rainbow variety of vegetables.

This summer I grew chili and banana peppers, which have been shown to have several health benefits. Another one that I am growing are tomatoes which are rich in antioxidants. Tomatoes contain potassium, vitamin C and are a source of fiber.

If you are like me and love pesto, you should try to grow basil. Basils are easy to care and grow inside or outside. Remember, basil can block calcium channels, which may help to lower blood pressure. It also contains magnesium, which can help to improve blood flow by allowing muscles and blood vessels to relax. Ask the herbal nursery in your neighborhood or check online to see how you could grow wonderful herbs in your zone area.

If you don't have the possibility to garden at home, keep in mind that community gardens are another option. By embracing your green thumb, you may be able to unpack your vegetable basket instead of a grocery bag.

The joy of seeing buds opening in spring is part of the therapy of gardening.

• **Art therapy**. Art is one of the best therapies ever which helps both adults and children to express their inner needs and desires, record the content of dreams and meditations. Art can be a key to the door of the inner mind, externalizing thoughts, feelings, and giving insight into hidden concerns that may be preventing a person from achieving full potential in life. I always like painting, even if I could not become a Picasso. I enjoy playing with colors and share my feelings of that moment in time. In a way, it is like journaling for me.

• **Music**. Music is therapy and a way of communication for millions of people in various cultures. There are many ways to gain access to music for healing purposes, the internet of course, has many resources of music and information.

Do yourself a favor and try to learn about music appreciation. There are classes you can take online. If you want to learn a new instrument, see what is practical and joyful for you then add it to your to do list.

Have fun with music. One of my recent birthdays, a friend of mine invited all for Karaoke. It was super fun, helped me unwind, and we all created a closer bond. It was a gathering that was also enjoyable for my mother to attend and watch.

• **Hydrotherapy.** Another favorite of mine therapy is being in the water. It can be ocean water, pool, jacuzzi, bathtub, or even showering. Being in the water calms me.

Since early times, water has been recognized as therapeutic. My grandmother owned a Persian Hammam in Tehran, Iran, which is a bath house where exfoliation of dead skin (called kisseh) with a shower mitt (called lief) was conducted using a special chalk like soap (called sephid ab). It was a ritual. Having tea, socializing with other women, relaxing, getting a massage, and pampering beauty time.

Many cultures have their version of hydrotherapy. I've also experienced the Korean spa, Turkish bath ritual, naturally flowing thermal mineral hot springs by the Arenal Volcano in Costa Rica, as well as thalassotherapy pools.

Thalassotherapy uses sea water. The sea has long been a source of healing and has been around for centuries. Seawater and blood plasma have an almost identical chemical composition, which makes seawater the perfect solution to replenish the body's minerals. You can find thalassotherapy pools on some cruise ships.

Swimming is a powerful form of exercise. I am one of the proofs of this that can help reduce stress levels, improve your mood, give you better sleep, increase your overall strength and increase your endurance and cardiovascular capacity. Any day that I swim, I sleep better at night and for some reason I feel that I can "let go" and be relaxed.

• **Aromatherapy.** Aromatherapy is thought to work by stimulating smell receptors in the nose, which then send messages through the nervous system to the limbic system—the part of the brain that controls emotions.

According to the NIH, aromatherapy is the use of essential oils from plants (flowers, herbs, or trees) as a complementary health approach. The essential oils are most often used by inhaling them or by applying a diluted form to the skin. Many essential oils are used in aromatherapy, including those from Roman chamomile, geranium, lavender, tea tree, lemon, ginger, cedarwood, and bergamot. Eucalyptus is my favorite because of the refreshing and awakening scent.

Essential oils used in aromatherapy are typically extracted from various parts of plants and then distilled. The highly concentrated oils may be inhaled directly or indirectly or applied to the skin through massage, lotions, or bath salts.

The therapeutic use of essential oils can be traced back thousands of years to the early Egyptian empire. Aromatherapy uses aromatic essential oils medicinally to improve the health of the body, mind, and spirit. It enhances both physical and emotional health. If you need improvement in health problems from anxiety to poor sleep, you may want to consider aromatherapy.

Some studies have shown that aromatherapy have these health benefits:
- Relief from anxiety and depression
- Reduced pain for people with kidney stones
- Reduced pain for people with osteoarthritis of the knee
- Improved quality of life, particularly for people with chronic health conditions
- Improved the quality of life for people with dementia
- Improved sleep

• **Mindfulness** - Did you know that mindfulness is one of the oldest and most basic skills known to mankind? It is learning and re-learning how to be present, how to be in the moment. It can be like stepping out of a gray flat-screen mode into a world that is vivid and three-dimensional.

Mindfulness means becoming more aware of what's going on right here, right now. We can appreciate our lives, instead of rushing through them, always trying to get somewhere else. The good news is that we can train ourselves in mindfulness, just as we exercise to keep our bodies healthy.

Now, you may ask if mindfulness is the same as meditation, and the answer is, no.

Mindfulness is a quality; meditation is a practice, and through this practice, one can develop different qualities, including mindfulness. Mindfulness describes a specific way of living that can be cultivated through practice.

I started my journey of practicing mindfulness with a monk at a temple. Mindfulness is a type of meditation in which you focus on being intensely aware of what you're sensing and feeling in the moment, without interpretation or judgment. Practicing mindfulness involves breathing methods, guided imagery, and other practices to relax the body and mind and helps reduce stress.

Spending too much time planning, problem-solving, daydreaming, or thinking negative or random thoughts can be draining and distracting. It can also make you more likely to experience stress, anxiety, and symptoms of depression. Practicing mindfulness exercises can help you direct your attention away from this kind of thinking and engage with the world around you.

Mindfulness is about teaching yourself to be more aware of your body, your mind, and the environment. It helps you with the following:

- Greater self-awareness and insight
- Being present at this moment; right here, right now, and to become more relaxed and calmer

- Being focused to make choices about where you place your attention
- Embodied being in your body, bringing your mind and your body into synch
- Accepting yourself and other people so to cope better with stress and anxiety
- Connect with a sense of the meaning of something bigger than self
- Enjoying and appreciating life more and having more sense of space in life

Remember that mindfulness is not a cure for the illness, but it has been shown to improve the body's ability to cope with a variety of physical conditions. Stress especially for family caregivers can weaken the response of the immune system, while evidence suggests mindfulness can strengthen it.

NIH performed a randomized, controlled study on the effects of the brain and immune function for a widely used eight-week clinical training program in mindfulness meditation applied in a work environment with healthy employees. The findings suggest that meditation may change brain and immune function in positive ways and underscores the need for additional research.

Mindfulness practice has been shown to have a calming effect on the nervous system, helping to switch off the stress response and bring us back into balance. We can take intelligent action rather than reacting blindly by losing our temper, overworking, or whatever else we tend to do.

Practicing mindfulness involves breathing methods to relax the body and mind and help reduce stress. It doesn't have to take long time to practice mindfulness. Even ten minutes a day can have a positive impact on your life. It will also strengthen your mindfulness muscles, so you'll find it much easier to become present throughout the day. You can do this when the loved one you take care of is taking a nap or doing word searches. It can take only for ten minutes—you can do it!

Practicing Mindfulness Breathing

Breathing is a natural object of meditation. By putting attention on your breath, you can change your state of consciousness, begin to relax, and detach from ordinary awareness. Many systems of meditation use focus on the breath as the main technique. In the Buddhist and yogic traditions are many examples of people who reached enlightenment by doing nothing other than paying attention to the rising and falling of their breath.

If today you can be aware of breathing for ten seconds more than you were yesterday, you will have taken a measurable step toward enlightenment, will have expanded your consciousness, furthered communication between mind and body, become a little more whole, and have improved your health. While diet and exercise are important, they are not the sole determinants of health. People who eat excellent diets and exercise faithfully are not always healthy, but the likelihood of being a healthy person who does not breathe well is slim.

CHAPTER 5 – YOUR PHYSICAL HEALTH

WE KNOW THAT TOO MUCH STRESS can infect every part of our lives and, there are times when our workouts may add even more. Think about those times when you set out to exercise only to spend the entire time clock-watching, rushing through your workout, and / or thinking about all the things you should be doing instead. Maybe your workouts feel so miserable, you deliberately distract yourself with anything you can get your hands on— your iPod, a TV, books, etc. When you aren't focused on what you're doing, you may lose that sense of satisfaction for a job well done and, not only that, but your workouts may also not be as effective.

Mindfulness Workout

Aim to practice mindfulness every day for about three months (90 days). Over time, you should find that mindfulness becomes effortless. Think of it as a commitment to reconnecting with and nurturing yourself. Here are some tips to get you started.

Many of us exercise to lose weight, but we must do it with purpose, something to work for, and to feel good about. For example, workout with purpose could be:

- "Today, I'm going to focus on chest and arm by 10-minute push-up"
- "Today, I'm going to do 5-minute squads"
- "Today, I'm doing cardio to burn calories and build endurance"

Take your time with each activity, especially with strength training exercises. Think about your posture, your core, and your muscle. See how much you can get out of your exercise time.

My recommendation, relax your mind and then consider starting with yoga or tai chi.

Yoga and Tai Chi

Yoga is an ancient form of exercise that focuses on strength, flexibility, and breathing to boost physical and mental well-being. The main components of yoga are postures (a series of movements designed to increase strength and flexibility) and breathing. Yoga is a system of self-improvement of conscious evolution that has itself evolved and modified over 6,000 years of its known existence. Yoga promotes not only physical mobility but a positive mental and emotional approach that can have profound psychological benefits.

Tai chi is only a few hundred years old. This Chinese martial art that combines movement and relaxation is good for both body and mind. It's been called "meditation in motion." Tai chi is made up of a series of graceful movements, one transitioning smoothly into the next. Take a class to help you get started and learn the proper form. You might find tai chi programs at your local YMCA, health club, community center, or senior center. Because tai chi also includes meditation and focused breathing, the researchers noted that tai chi may be superior to other forms of exercise for reducing stress and anxiety.

The main difference between yoga and tai chi is execution. Yoga involves holding poses and postures. Tai chi is performed in a dance-like, martial arts form. Both can be rigorous, or low impact, depending on the person's fitness level.

No matter your age or fitness level, these activities are some of the best exercises you can do and will help you get in shape and lower your risk for disease.

Another study in *Scientific American* by Brock Armstrong on November 15, 2018, stated that sixty-two women over six months found that those who applied mindfulness meditation practices to their daily or weekly routine had a much higher level of physical exercise and general movement, and a greater reduction in BMI, than those who didn't employ mindfulness practices.

Tips to Practice Mindfulness Right Now

Did you know that you can exercise and meditate at the same time?

The two practices are even stronger together. Both exercise and meditation have been touted as great ways to reduce anxiety and depression. Together, these two might just be the best combination since peanut butter and jelly.

- Stop what you're doing and take a breath.
- Take a moment to notice the sensation of your breath.

Simple Meditation Exercises

A meditation exercise can be as simple as doing some deep breathing or repeating a mantra or as complex in doing transcendental meditation. Any activity that helps to quiet the mind could be considered a meditative activity, even sitting outside and quietly watching the birds or the world go by.

Besides yoga and tai chi workouts, there are other activities requiring physical effort for improving health and fitness. All you need is a well-fitting and supportive pair of shoes. Start with walking for about ten to fifteen minutes at a time. Over time, you can start to walk farther and faster, until you're walking for thirty to sixty minutes on most days of the week.

Another activity that I recommend is stretching. Stretching is a form of physical exercise in which a specific muscle or tendon (or muscle group) is deliberately flexed or stretched to improve the muscle's felt elasticity and achieve comfortable muscle tone. The result is a feeling of increased muscle control, flexibility, and range of motion.

In the following image, I have outlined some simple stretches you can do. Some of these you can also do in a chair or even standing while using a wall for support. For advanced methods you can use a yoga ball. Set a time aside (8AM or 10PM) and do as much as possible (sets of 3 for each are ideal), just get started and start feeling good today.

Image 5-1 Simple Exercise Stretches

Additional Exercises Combining the Emotional and Physical

• **Resistance Bands Workout** – Resistance bands do build muscle and I am truly a fan of them, because resistance bands are great for those who want to exercise at home, or who like to take their workouts along when they travel, like my daughter. Resistance band exercises are surprisingly effective and offer many benefits over traditional free weights. Though free weights, like dumbbells for women, have always been the go-to for muscle-building, resistance bands can be equally effective at building both strength and muscle mass.

• **Dancing** – My other favorite is dancing. It is fun and a great exercise. I consider it as a cardio activity to improve balance and strength and great for challenging your brain. Dancing helps to build stronger bones and reduces the risk of osteoporosis. Dancing can be a social activity and improves your mood.

• **Ice Skating** – I love to skate. Two years ago, I thought I could not do it anymore. However, I learned that there are walkers for the ice rink to help with balance. There are a lot of health benefits to ice skating, such as burning calories, building muscles, strengthening your joints, building up your mood, and of course improving your balance.

• **Horseback Riding** – Luckily, I live in the suburbs, and there are stables that I could go to once a week in the spring and fall to do some light riding. It has helped me to consciously improve my posture. Additionally, spending time with animals and exercising releases a hormone called serotonin, which can improve your mood and reduce your stress levels.

• **Kayaking** – Kayaking is another my favorite summer activity that I love to do in good weather. Many areas in the U.S. are packed with plentiful kayaking adventures, from scenic canals and ponds to leaf-shaded creeks, to broad expanses of inland bay. Can you imagine the feeling of paddling in the water, surrounded by beautiful birds? You feel amazing and improve strengthening your arm muscles. You can easily burn hundreds of calories during a couple hours of kayaking. It will be a memorable time if you do it with a friend.

• **Biking** – When I can I bike to the grocery stores, to the bank, to pick up my mail, and our local farmers. Since biking has super health benefits, we should not ignore indoor cycling in a gym or at home when we cannot bike outside. The other health benefits include decreasing body fat and stress levels as well as improving joint mobility and posture.

• **Playing Tennis or Pickleball.** When I was younger, tennis was the best exercise I can remember. Fortunately, I recently learned about pickleball through my friends in my community. It really felt good to play. My children have now joined me, and my son has been teaching my daughter and I some of the rules. It has been a great bonding time for me and the family. My mother is there sitting, watching, and sometimes walking around safely with her walker helping us pick up the balls. For me it is a great substitute and fun to play with friends and family.

• **Golfing** – If you have access to it, practice it. Because golf is a leisurely sport, many people don't think of it as promoting heart health. Conversely, since it is easygoing, injuries are believed to be rare. These health benefits don't come from swinging your club, but from walking.

• **Gardening** – As you can see in almost every chapter of this book, I mention gardening. It is really fulfilling to garden and creates an activity you can have the one you are caring for join in on.

Starting a garden is one of the healthiest choices you can make and a great way to get fresh fruits and vegetables into your daily diet. Gardening just makes me happy. I have downloaded apps to learn more about the plants and how to care for them. Plus, it is something I share and discuss with my neighbors. We all learn from each other and share what we grow. This activity makes me calm and gives me amazing satisfaction. My plan is to add more to my collection like strawberry, blueberry, and lavender. I look forward to the springtime and thinking of my future gardening landscape.

CHAPTER 6 – NUTRITION FOR A HEALTHY LIFESTYLE

NUTRITION IS THE STUDY OF components in foods, called nutrients, and how they are ingested, digested, absorbed, transported, and used, including how they interact and how they are stored and excreted, as defined by the US Department of Health.

Nutrition is a critical part of health and development. Better nutrition is related to an improved and stronger immune system and lowers the risk of non-communicable diseases (such as diabetes and cardiovascular disease.) Eating the right foods can help your body cope more successfully with an ongoing illness. Understanding good nutrition and paying attention to what you eat can help you maintain or improve your health.

According to Healthline.com, good nutrition also involves avoiding certain kinds of foods. Sodium is used heavily in processed foods and is dangerous for people with high blood pressure. The USDA advises adults to consume less than 300 milligrams (mg) per day of cholesterol (found in meat and full-fat dairy products among others.) Fried food, solid fats, and trans fats found in margarine and processed foods can be harmful to heart health. Refined grains (white flour, white rice) and refined sugar (table sugar, high fructose corn syrup) are also bad for long-term health, especially in people with diabetes. Alcohol can be dangerous to health in amounts more than one serving per day for a woman and two per day for a man.

There are many high-quality, free guidelines available for healthy eating plans that give more details on portion size, total calorie consumption, what to eat more of, and what to eat less of to get healthy and stay that way.

Because a healthy diet will mean making new habits, think about where you'll start. A good way to start a new habit is to take the first few steps. Begin with drinking beverages at each meal and two or three times between meals. Examples of healthy drinks include water, milk, and non-sweetened drinks.

A healthy diet includes a lot of natural foods. A sizeable portion of a healthy diet should consist of fruits and vegetables, especially ones that are red, orange, or dark green. Whole grains, such as whole wheat and brown rice, should also play a part in your diet. For adults, dairy products should be nonfat or low-fat.

I created a rule of 7 to make it easy to remember how to eat healthier. I know it seems like a big list, but these are important to know and very essential knowledge for your healthy lifestyle. It is a reference that you can use and has been collected from accredited sources.

The NIH defines the six major nutrients: proteins, carbohydrates (cho), lipids (fats), vitamins, minerals, water. I added fiber because it is an important nutrient that may promote weight loss, lower blood sugar levels, and fight constipation. Let's look at each one in more depth.

Rule of 7 for Healthier Eating
1. Proteins

As a nutrient, protein performs many functions in the body. An adequate dietary protein intake is important for building, maintaining, and repairing body tissues. The body's structural components, such as skin, muscles, bones, and organs, are made up in large part by protein.

Ways you can add protein to your day include:

- Include high-protein food like fish, chicken, beef, eggs with every meal
- Snack on cheese (choose cottage cheese)
- Top your salad with chopped almonds
- Add oats to your Greek yogurt
- Have a protein shake

2. Carbohydrates

Carbohydrates are the sugars, starches, and fibers found in fruits, grains, vegetables, and milk products. A food that contains 15 grams of carbohydrate is called "one carb serving." For example, one slice of bread, a small piece of fruit, a small apple contains 21 grams of carbs.

Food that has carbs include the following: most dairy, fruits, grains, legumes, starchy vegetable (potato and corn), cereal with lots of sugar.

3. Fats

Fats are essential for your body functions and your health. There are fats that are good for you, and as long as the fat comes from whole foods and not processed ones. Here are some high-fat foods that are incredibly healthy and nutritious.

- Avocados
- Cheese
- Whole eggs
- Fatty fish
- Nuts
- Extra-virgin olive oil

4. Vitamins

Vitamins are organic substances made by plants and animals, which are then eaten by humans. Here are the essential vitamins:

The Essential Vitamins

- **Vitamin A**: An antioxidant that helps protect the cells from cancers, vitamin A is essential for eye health and can be found in produce like carrots, sweet potatoes, and dark leafy greens.

  The top food sources of vitamin A in the U.S. diet include dairy products, liver, fish, and fortified cereals; the top sources of provitamin A includes carrots, broccoli, cantaloupe, and squash.

- **Vitamin B-Complex:**
  - **Vitamin B2**: B2 better known as riboflavin, vitamin B2 helps turn sugar, fat, and protein into energy.
  - **Vitamin B3**: B3 Better known as niacin, this vitamin helps balance sugar and cholesterol levels in the blood. It also helps with energy production and brain function.
  - **Vitamin B5**: Also known as pantothenic acid, vitamin B5 is also involved in energy production and the metabolism of fats. It is essential for brain and nerve function and helps in the production of steroid hormones. This essential vitamin is also a natural antidepressant and diuretic.
  - **Vitamin B6**: Also known as pyridoxine, is a water-soluble vitamin that your body needs for several functions. It's significant to protein, fat, and carbohydrate metabolism and the creation of red blood cells and neurotransmitters. Your body cannot produce vitamin B6, so you must obtain it from foods or supplements.

o **Vitamin B7**: Vitamin B7, also called biotin, is a vital part of a healthy metabolism and creating important enzymes. Biotin is often used to strengthen hair, nails, and is also called vitamin H (for hair). Other benefits of biotin include the skin, nerves, digestive tract, metabolism, and cells.

o **Vitamin B12**: This well-known vitamin carries oxygen through the body and is essential for energy production, the synthesis of DNA, and proper nerve function. It plays a crucial role in metabolizing folic acid, which is important for the developing brain and nervous system, as well as for red blood cell formation. Other B vitamins are thiamin, riboflavin, niacin, pantothenic acid, biotin, and folate.

o **Vitamin H (Biotin)**: Vitamin H more commonly known as biotin is part of the B-complex group of vitamins. All B vitamins help the body to convert food (carbohydrates) into fuel (glucose), which is used to produce energy. These B vitamins often referred to as B-complex vitamins, also help the body metabolize fats and protein.

Vitamin H (the H represents Haar und Haut, German words for hair and skin), vitamin B7, or vitamin B8 (in many countries like France, where vitamin B7 is used for inositol) is a water-soluble B vitamin.

Some fruits, vegetables, dairy products, and whole grains contain biotin. Eggs and some organ meats are good sources of biotin; many nuts, seeds, seafood, and lean meats contain biotin.

7 Best Food Sources of Vitamin B
- Whole grains (brown rice, barley, millet)
- Meat (red meat, poultry, fish)
- Eggs and dairy products (milk, cheese)
- Legumes (beans, lentils)
- Seeds and nuts (sunflower seeds, almonds)
- Dark, leafy vegetables (broccoli, spinach)
- Fruits (citrus fruits, avocados, bananas)

- **Vitamin C**: Vitamin C is necessary for the growth, development, and repair of all body tissues. It's involved in many body functions, including the formation of collagen, absorption of iron, the immune system, wound healing, and the maintenance of cartilage, bones, and teeth.

Vitamin C has been shown in many studies to have preventive value in the common cold. The nutrient is featured in supplements promising to boost the immune system.

According to WebMD, foods with vitamin C besides oranges are red pepper, kiwifruit, broccoli, cantaloupe, tomatoes, and potato. You only need 500 to 1,000 mg per day, no more!

Vitamin C lasts only a few hours in the bloodstream and should be replaced throughout the day. Very high doses of vitamin C are known to cause gastric discomfort and diarrhea. Avoid taking vitamin C before bedtime.

- **Vitamin D**: In promoting healthy bones, largely by promoting the absorption of calcium, vitamin D is necessary for building and maintaining healthy bones. That's because calcium, the primary component of bone, can only be absorbed by your body when vitamin D is present. Your body makes vitamin D when direct sunlight converts a chemical in your skin into an active form of the vitamin (calciferol, or D2).

  Vitamin D is best absorbed when taken with a meal containing fats or oils. For example, fish oil can help with that. Vitamin D is found more tuna, salmon, orange juice, soy milk, cheese, and egg yolk.

- **Vitamin E**: Vitamin E is a nutrient that's important to vision, reproduction, and the health of your blood, brain, and skin. Vitamin E deficiency can cause nerve pain (neuropathy). The recommended daily amount of vitamin E for adults is 15 milligrams a day. Vitamin E also has antioxidant properties.

  You could get your vitamin E from canola oil, olive oil, margarine, almonds, peanuts, and leafy greens.

- **Vitamin K**: Vitamin K plays a key role in helping the blood clot, preventing excessive bleeding. Unlike many other vitamins, vitamin K is not typically used as a dietary supplement. Vitamin K is mainly found in plant-sourced foods, especially dark, leafy green vegetables (such as kale, spinach, broccoli), kiwi, prunes, and blueberries.

Water-soluble vitamins are B and C. The rest of the vitamins are fat-soluble. Fat-soluble vitamins don't immediately leave the body. Instead, they're stored in the liver or fatty tissue for later use. They are found in high-fat food sources like egg yolks, liver, beef, fatty fish, and dairy products.

Our intestines absorb certain vitamins—vitamin A, D, E, and K—when they're paired with a fat source. Getting enough of these vitamins and maximally absorbing them is important because deficiencies relate to a heightened risk of cancer and type 2 diabetes.

5. Minerals

Major minerals needed by your body include calcium, chloride, magnesium, phosphorus, potassium, sodium, sulfur, and iron. Minerals help your body grow, develop, and stay healthy.

You can find minerals in food like:

- Meat and fish
- Cereals
- Milk
- Dairy foods
- Fruit
- Vegetables
- Nuts

The Vitamin and Mineral Partnership

Our vitamins and minerals work together to keep us healthy. In this section, we will explore some of the more common relationships.

According to the Office of Dietary Supplements (ODS) of the National Institutes of Health (NIH):

- **Calcium and Vitamin D** work together to protect your bones—calcium helps build and maintain bones, while vitamin D helps your body effectively absorb calcium. So, even if you're taking in enough calcium, it could be going to waste if you're deficient in vitamin D.

- As **vitamin B and magnesium** don't affect each other's absorption inside your body, you'll find that many supplements combine the two. Like with magnesium, your body can't store vitamin B—it's water-soluble, which means it dissolves in water—and so it needs to top up its supply each day.

7 Nutrients to Take Together for Best Absorption

The following combinations of nutrients were collected from the Mayo Clinic, the Office of Dietary Supplements (ODS) and WebMD:

- Vitamin D + Calcium
- Vitamin D + Healthy Fats
- Vitamin B12 + Folate (also known as folic acid or vitamin B9)
- Vitamin D + Omega-3s
- Vitamin E + Vitamin K
- Iron + Vitamin C
- Iron + Copper + Zinc

A few years ago, for several weeks, I was so tired. I would sleep good at night, however throughout the day, I needed to nap many different times. Fortunately, I knew about iron. I asked my doctor to test my iron level. I was right! I was deficient in my iron level and needed to take iron supplement. Not everyone needs that, because too much iron can lead to life-threatening conditions, such as liver disease, heart problems and diabetes. Always consult with your doctor before taking any supplement. Iron is best absorbed on an empty stomach. Yet, iron supplements can cause stomach cramps, nausea, and diarrhea in some people. You may need to take iron with a small amount of food to avoid this problem. Milk, calcium, and antacids should NOT be taken at the same time as iron supplements.

Supplement Insight

The most popular nutrient supplements are multivitamins, calcium, and vitamins B, C, and D. Calcium supports bone health, and vitamin D helps the body absorb calcium. Vitamins C and E are antioxidants—molecules that prevent cell damage and help to maintain health.

I needed iron but I made sure I did not take them with calcium such as milk. Plus, I needed to be conscious to take my iron pill in the afternoon, several hours after my multivitamins in the morning.

It's possible to get all of the nutrients you need by eating a variety of healthy foods, so you don't have to take one. Vitamin B12 keeps nerve and blood cells healthy. Vitamin B12 mostly comes from meat, fish, and dairy foods, so vegans may consider taking a supplement to be sure to get enough of it.

> Speak to your health care providers about your vitamin, mineral, and supplement intake, and cross check what not to mix with others.

6. Water

Water is the main constituent of the body and forms 50-60% of body weight. Water contains no fats, no proteins, no carbohydrates, and therefore no calories. The water-soluble vitamins— C and the B-complex vitamins (such as vitamins B6, B12, niacin, riboflavin, and folate) — need to dissolve in water before your body can absorb them.

Health authorities like, the U.S. Department of Health and Human Services (HHS) and the Centers for Disease Control and Prevention (CDC), commonly recommend you to be drinking eight (8-ounce) glasses every day. Which equals about two liters, or half a gallon. This is called the 8×8 rule and is very easy to remember.

Water is a nutrient all in its own. Helping every cell in your body to function properly. Most people get about 20% of their water through food and the rest by drinking water or other beverages. Bottled mineral water may also contain these and other minerals, including sodium. Read bottle labels or request tap-water reports from your city to learn the exact mineral content of your drinking water.

7 Nutrients in Drinking Good Water

- **Calcium**—important for bone health and possibly cardiovascular health.
- **Magnesium**—important for bone and cardiovascular health.
- **Sodium**—an important extracellular electrolyte, lost under conditions of excess sweat.
- **Copper**—important in antioxidant function, iron utilization, and cardiovascular health.
- **Selenium**—important in the general antioxidant function and the immune system.
- **Potassium**—important for a variety of biochemical effects (but it is usually not found in natural drinking water at significant levels)
- **Fluoride**—Most drinking water naturally contains fluoride, and many cities and towns add fluoride to the water supply to help promote stronger teeth.

7. Dietary Fiber

The Academy of Nutrition and Dietetics recommends 30 to 38 grams of dietary fiber each day for men and 21 to 25 grams for women. Foods containing fiber can provide other health benefits as well, such as helping maintain a healthy weight and lowering your risk of diabetes, heart disease, and some types of cancer.

High-Fiber Foods:

- Fiber-rich fruits include bananas, oranges, apples, mangoes, strawberries, raspberries.
- Generally, the darker the vegetable color, the higher the fiber content.
- Beans and legumes are flavorful, fiber-filled additions to salads, soups, and chilis.
- Bread and grains
- Nuts

Best Fruits to Support Your Major Organs

Did you know that there are seventy-eight main organs within the human body? Among these 78 organs, seven organs are considered as vital for survival. These are the brain, heart, kidneys, liver, lungs, pancreas, and skin. The human brain is the body's control center, receiving and sending signals to other organs through the nervous system and through secreted hormones.

Seven top fruits that support your major organs:

- **Blackberries** may improve **brain** health and help prevent memory loss caused by aging.
- **Strawberries** are **heart**-healthy and packed with vitamin C, fiber, antioxidants, and more.

SELF-CARE FOR FAMILY CAREGIVERS

- **Red Grapes** are the fruits for people who want healthy **lungs**.
- **Pineapple** makes a sweet, low-potassium alternative for those with **kidney** problems.
- **Pomegranate** is an antioxidant and anti-inflammatory and it could be considered as a good candidate alternative medicine with beneficial effects on the **pancreas**.
- **Prickly Pear** is commonly used in traditional medicine to treat **liver** disease, fatigue, and ulcers.
- **Kiwi** fruits have a high concentration of antioxidants, such as vitamin C and vitamin E. Though kiwi is delicious as a snack, it also has benefits when applied directly to the **skin**.

Top Healthy Nuts

You know you need to eat your fruits and veggies and that whole grains are good for you. But you might be missing out on another hugely beneficial food group: nuts. Nuts are nature's perfect snack, packed with protein, healthy fats, and antioxidants. Here I share what nuts can do for your health and which ones offer the best benefits.

Not sure which ones to choose? Here's a list of some of the healthiest nuts.

• **Walnuts** - In 2020 NIH reported that substantial evidence from animal and human studies suggests that dietary consumption of walnuts (1 to 2 oz per day) can improve cognitive function and reduce the risk of other diseases, such as cardiovascular disease, depression, and type 2 diabetes, which are risk factors for the development of dementia.

Walnuts are one of the ultimate superfoods, with evidence showing that they play a role in improving heart health, protecting the brain—they may even help fight breast and prostate cancers. A 2011 analysis suggested that walnuts have higher quality of antioxidants than any other nut, making them hugely powerful against inflammation. Some research has shown that walnuts could help prevent Alzheimer's, and one study even found that walnuts help the body better deal with stress. Another bonus? Because of the way your body breaks down the nuts, you'll get about 20% fewer calories from walnuts than it says on the label.

• **Almonds** – A small serving of almonds offers lots of healthy fats and fiber, including the kind that acts as prebiotics, feeding the healthy bacteria in your gut. The Institute of Food Research (ITF) found that eating almonds can increase levels of microbes that improve your digestive health. which are notoriously high in vitamin E and contain polyphenols, have an important antioxidant effect, even when eaten in small amounts. The combination of antioxidants, healthy fats, and fiber is thought to promote heart health, lowering cholesterol levels, reducing blood pressure, and improving blood flow.

• **Pistachios** – When you eat pistachios, your heart will thank you. Not only are they filled with heart-healthy fats, but they've also been linked to healthy cholesterol levels, and they contain resveratrol, the same anti-inflammatory that is found in red wine. Eating nuts, in general, has been linked to controlling type 2 diabetes, but pistachios have been shown to help maintain healthy glucose levels and reduce the effects of stress on the heart in people who suffer from diabetes. And if you have trouble with portion control when it comes to nuts, pistachios are likely the best nut for you. They are lower in calories than most varieties and the process of taking the shell off will help slow you down as you eat.

• **Pecans** – Pecans are another leader among high-antioxidant foods. With vitamin E and ellagic acid, both anti-inflammatory nutrients, these nuts have plenty of health-boosting powers, including fighting some cancers. These antioxidants prevent lipid oxidation in the blood, which can reduce buildup in the arteries. All those antioxidants can also benefit the skin, fighting free radical damage to help keep your complexion radiant.

• **Brazil Nuts** - Like walnuts, Brazil nuts offer lots of omega-3s, which are super healthy for the heart. These fats, as well as the mineral zinc, which is found in Brazil nuts, have been associated with healthy, clear skin. These nuts are also a very good source of selenium, which has been associated with fighting bladder, lung, and prostate cancers, to name a few. Like most nuts, the Brazil nut is also touted as great food for weight loss—it has a rich, satisfying flavor and is very filling. Just don't overdo it, as these nuts are high in calories.

• **Peanuts** - These legumes (that's right; they're not technically a nut!) have gotten a bad rap over the years, largely due to sugary peanut butter and allergies associated with them. But the truth is, if you aren't allergic, peanuts have a lot to offer. Eating peanuts can help triglyceride levels (which are associated with your cholesterol and overall heart health), and their monounsaturated fats are great for your heart. Research has linked eating peanuts to a lower risk for gallstones and protection against Alzheimer's disease.

• **Cashews** - These nuts have a rich and buttery flavor but are lower in fat than most other nuts. The fat they do contain is the heart-healthy monounsaturated variety. Plus, they've got a good dose of magnesium, which is important for strong bones. Research has shown that eating cashews, and other nuts might help decrease your risk of gallstones. And they contain lots of essential minerals, including selenium, copper, and zinc.

Tea and Its Value

Tea is second only to water as the world's most popular beverage. Camellia sinensis (or tea plant) is used to make most traditional caffeinated teas, including black tea, white tea, oolong tea, and green tea. This plant originated near the southwest region of China as an evergreen forest shrub. Green tea has long been valued as a stimulant to control bleeding and help heal wounds and a tonic for improving the condition of the heart and blood vessels. Once you have dried your herbs, they are ready to use right away, but more often you will want to store the herbs for later. They may last for 6 to 12 months, but the sooner you use them, the more flavor you will have.

The antioxidants and vitamins found in herbal teas are great for helping fight disease and infections, protect against oxidative stress, and lower the risk of chronic disease.

Did you know that white, green, oolong, black and dark tea are all products of Camellia Sinensis leaves and buds? The only difference is how they are processed. You can turn the fresh plucked green tea leaves into any of the varieties. White tea is minimally processed. Oolong is fermented and allowed to partially oxidize, while green tea is not. Black tea is fully fermented and oxidized, which gives it the characteristic color black.

Studies have found that some teas may help with cancer, heart disease, and diabetes; encourage weight loss; lower cholesterol, and bring about mental alertness. Tea also appears to have antimicrobial qualities.

- Black tea is good for your heart and may help reduce cholesterol levels. And it can also help boost your energy levels.
- Green tea is packed with good-for-you antioxidants that may keep you in great form long-term. It may also help fight certain diseases.

- White or green tea may help with weight loss, thanks to caffeine and antioxidants called catechins.
- Oolong tea may not be as well-known as green or black tea, but it has similar health benefits. These include benefits for heart, brain, bone, and dental health.

My children bought me a few years ago a tea brewing machine. I enter the type of tea, (black, white, oolong, green), and the machine takes care of the rest.

Herbal Teas

Herbal teas come from soaking various flowers, leaves, or spices in hot water. Most of these brews do not have caffeine.

Drinking a tea brewed from freshly gathered herbs is an easy way to get nature's healing force into your body, something we all need, whether we are healthy or fighting illness. Fresh or dried plants help strengthen the immune system and detoxify. They are loaded with vitamins, antioxidants, essential oils, soluble fiber, minerals, enzymes, chlorophyll, and numerous compounds to boost our health.

Herbal teas have lower concentrations of antioxidants than green, white, black, and oolong teas. Their chemical compositions vary widely depending on the plant used.

Top Healthy Herbal Teas:
- Chamomile
- Sage
- Dandelion
- Daisy
- Lemon Balm
- Peppermint
- Hibiscus

• **Chamomile** - Chamomile remains a popular treatment for digestive and inflammatory conditions. In modern herbal medicine, it is suggested for indigestion, heartburn, diarrhea, and irritable bowel syndrome. It is recommended to relieve muscle tension and to ease anxiety.

• **Sage** - Sage is native to the Mediterranean region. It grows in Spain, Italy, and France. Nowadays, you can easily grow it in your garden or at home since you can buy it at supermarkets almost anywhere in the world.

Fresh sage leaves can be laid directly on wounds, which will then heal better and faster. Sage tea can help ease stomach pain, prevents and heals stomach ulcers, and is an excellent herb for sore throat.

• **Dandelion** - Dandelions are well-known, robust weeds; the common name derives from the French "dent de lion," meaning "lion's tooth," which refers to the deeply toothed, dark green leaves, which are arranged in rosettes. The bright-yellow flower head (open in the daytime but closed at night) is borne on a single hollow stem.

Vitamins are abundant, especially A, B2, C, and D. Some minerals include amino acids, sodium, potassium, manganese, sulfur, and phosphorus.

Dandelion leaves should ideally be harvested from May to September. Turn the leaves over several times while drying, and if dried properly, the leaves of the dandelion should keep their fresh green color. If they darken, they cannot be used.

The leaves help to relieve swelling, cleanse the liver, digestive tract, and relieve heartburn symptoms.

• **Daisy** - The common daisy is native to Europe and western Asia but has now been naturalized in many parts of the globe. Its tea is famed to relieve coughs, dissolve mucous, and cleansing the airway.

Diabetics will appreciate the fact that the daisy can also lower blood sugar.

• **Lemon Balm** - In modern herbal medicine, lemon balm is combined with other calming herbs, such as valerian to reduce anxiety and promote sleep. Recent studies indicate that it may also improve secondary memory and the ability to learn and retrieve information.

Hence, herbal practitioners recommend lemon balm for Alzheimer's disease, dementia, and attention-deficit/hyperactivity disorder (ADHD).

• **Peppermint** - Peppermint tea is a popular herbal tea that is naturally calorie and caffeine-free.

Top Health Benefits of Peppermint Tea

- Relieves digestive symptoms, such as gas, bloating, and indigestion.
- Helps relieve tension headaches and migraines.
- Freshens your breath.
- Relieves clogged sinuses.
- Improves energy.
- Fights bacterial infections.
- Improves your sleep.

• **Hibiscus** - Hibiscus tea has been known to prevent hypertension, lower blood pressure, reduce blood sugar levels, keep your liver healthy, help with menstrual cramps, depression, aid digestion, and weight management. It's rich in vitamin C, contains minerals such as flavonoids, and has laxative properties.

A small study found that drinking three cups of hibiscus tea daily lowered blood pressure in people with modestly elevated levels.

Instructions to Make a Cup of Herbal Tea:

Pour 1 cup boiling water over 1 teaspoon of herb. Steep for 5 to 7 minutes. The longer steeps, the more powerful it becomes.

Teatime's Benefits: Being Social and Spending Time with Others

I well remember my great-grandmother had a teatime ceremony every afternoon. Friends and family would come for a visit and have small bites of food. My favorite calming tea was the borage tea (in Persia it is called "Gol Gov Zaban".)

Persians usually have afternoon tea between 3:30 and 5:00 p.m., and 4:00 p.m. is often cited as the best time for afternoon tea in Europe and the UK as well. Many hotels and restaurants offer it from noon until early evening, though, so you don't have to stick to the rules if you want to have it earlier or later. This is an old tradition in Europe and the Middle East, and I truly liked it. This is a perfect idea for family caregivers to have a me time.

In British afternoon tea etiquette, one must eat the sandwiches first, and with fingers, not cutlery. The scones should still be warm. Scones should be cut in two by hand, not with a knife, and each half should be eaten separately.

One of my most favorite ways to spend time with friends and family is the afternoon teatime. Teatime gives you a chance to catch up with friends and family without distractions. It is about embracing the simplicity of the moment and the conversation of the people you are with.

Staying mindful is an important skill that has health-improving benefits, so you should feel good about carving out time for a warm cup of tea. It can help you stay mindful. I believe every step of the way with fine tea can be an everyday luxury.

Now that we understand how to support our emotions, physical body, and get the nutrition for our healthy lifestyle, the next chapter is about improving our healthier and happier life through prevention.

CHAPTER 7 – PREVENTION IS THE KEY

YOU'VE HEARD THE EXPRESSION, "knowledge is power," right? The more you know, the more power you have to achieve your goal which now is adapting to a new healthy lifestyle for yourself as a family caregiver. Preventing yourself from getting sick, physically, and emotionally is the key.

We all get sick. And we will get sick again. But isn't it better to prevent it by understanding our physical health? It is possible to get sick regularly when the immune system is not functioning correctly because the body is unable to fight off germs properly. If an infection occurs, it can take longer than usual to recover.

Before we get to the list of matters to our health, let's have a basic knowledge about our body. I read this somewhere and I think it is good way to learn about our immune system; like white knights slaying a dragon, white blood cells charge into battle at any sign of trouble? These brave soldiers only live up to a few weeks, but your bone marrow is always making them and it's a good thing that there's a lot of them—a single drop of blood can contain up to 25,000 white blood cells. White blood cells are part of the body's immune system. They help the body fight infection and other diseases. They are made in your bone, and they move through blood and tissue throughout your body, looking for foreign invaders (microbes) such as bacteria, viruses, and fungi, and when they find them, they launch an immune attack.

Eating vitamin C will help regulate the levels of white blood cells in your body. Fruits like lemons, oranges, and lime are rich in vitamin C, and so are papayas, berries, guavas, and pineapples. You can also get vitamin C from vegetables such as cauliflower, broccoli, carrots, and bell peppers.

Do You Know Why We Get Sick?

Being sick is part of our life. Same as feeling well. Yet, how is it possible to have more well days than sick days?

First, you must know what's making you sick. There are many different reasons that causes our sickness. I share more in the following section.

Six Reasons We Get Sick

1. Immune System Disorder
2. Lack of Vitamin D
3. Dehydration
4. Dirty Hands
5. Lack of Iron
6. Lack of Protein

Let's talk about them:

1. **Immune System Disorders** - Immune system disorders occur when a person's immune system doesn't fight antigens. Antigens are harmful substances, including, bacteria, toxins, cancer cells, viruses, fungi, allergens such as pollen, and foreign blood tissues.

   Some people have immune systems that don't work as well as they should. These immune systems can't produce effective antibodies to prevent illness.

Your immune system is ready for anything you can throw at it. But it can only handle so much. Stress has a significant effect on your immune system. During stress, a series of events release cortisol, adrenaline, and other stress hormones from the adrenal gland. Together, they help your body cope with stress. Normally, cortisol is helpful because it decreases the inflammation in the body that results from the immune responses caused by stress.

I picked these seven foods to highlight because we should use them often to support our immune systems. They should be easy to access, and we can eat them for snacks as well as meals: leafy greens, red bell peppers, broccoli, nuts and seeds, berries, mangoes, and kiwi.

2. **Lack of Vitamin D** - Increase your vitamin D intake with foods like fatty fish, egg yolks, and mushrooms. Go outside for 10–15 minutes each day to reap the benefits of the "sunshine vitamin."

3. **Dehydration** - Every tissue and organ within the body depends on water. It helps carry nutrients and minerals to cells, and keeps your mouth, nose, and throat moist—important for avoiding illness. Even though the body is made up of 60% water, you lose fluids through urination, bowel movements, sweating, and even breathing. Dehydration occurs when you don't adequately replace the fluids you lose. Dehydration can be dangerous, even life-threatening. Symptoms can include, extreme thirst, sunken eyes, headache, low blood pressure or hypotension, and fast heartbeat.

The treatment is simple: it is very important that during your day to drink 6-8 glass of water, especially in hot or humid conditions. Eating foods with a high-water content, such as fruits and vegetables, also keeps you hydrated throughout the day.

ELLIE NAZEMOFF

4. **Dirty Hands** - Your hands come into contact with many germs throughout the day. When you don't wash your hands regularly, and then touch your face, lips, or your food, you can spread illnesses. You can even infect yourself. Simply washing your hands with running water and antibacterial soap for 20 seconds helps you stay healthy and avoid illness-causing bacteria.

5. **Lack of Iron** - Iron deficiency means less oxygen is being delivered to the hands and feet. Some people may feel the cold more easily in general or have cold hands and feet. Talk with your doctor to discuss the intake of iron supplement for your body.

6. **Lack of Protein** - Your muscles, skin, hair, bones, and blood are largely made of protein. For this reason, protein deficiency has a wide range of symptoms. Serious protein deficiency can cause swelling, fatty liver, and skin degeneration.

Common Symptoms and Their Therapies

Now that you know the reasons for sickness, here I share the common symptoms and their therapies:

- Cold and flu
- Infection
- Cough
- Sleep deficiency
- Allergies
- Headaches
- Depression

80

• **Cold and Flu** - Common Cold and Flu Symptoms include sneezing, watery eyes, scratchy throat, cough, swollen glands in the neck, stuffy or runny nose, thirst, and mild fever. The common cold is caused by droplet infection since the virus is usually passed from person to person via droplets in the air or droplets passed from hand to hand and hand to mouth.

According to the CDC, flu and the common cold are both respiratory illnesses but are caused by different viruses.

Therapies for Cold and Flu: Sprinkling a drop of eucalyptus oil on a tissue and inhaling it helps to unblock a stuffy nose. Hot tea of peppermint is beneficial too. Drink at least three times a day.

• **Infection** - One of the major tasks of the immune system is the detection, interception, and elimination of infectious agents. There are two main sources of infection: bacteria and virus.

Therapies for Infection: Antibiotic drugs are conventional therapies provided by your doctor. Major natural antibiotic remedies include garlic, honey, turmeric, ginger, oregano.

• **Cough** - Coughing is stimulated by anything that activates the cough reflex. Cough is a symptom for a disease, such as chronic obstructive pulmonary disease (COPD), asthma or pulmonary fibrosis. It is not just part of a cold or flu.

Therapies for Cough: The juice of aloe vera mixed with an equal part of honey is particularly good for scratchy coughs. Vitamins A, C, E, and zinc are helpful in conditions that cause coughing. A bath or shower that creates lots of steam can ease coughing, and hot packs applied to the throat or chest are soothing.

Antibiotics for infection and drugs for coughing are suggested as conventional therapies.

• **Sleep Deficiency** - Sleep is one of the most natural functions in the cycle of life, yet millions of us seem to have great difficulty with it. Some of the most serious potential problems associated with chronic sleep deprivation are high blood pressure, type 2 diabetes, heart attack, heart failure, stroke, obesity, and depression that threaten our nation's health.

Other potential problems include obesity, depression, impairment in immunity, and lower sex drive. Chronic sleep deprivation can even affect your appearance.

Insomnia is the biggest sleep problem of all. Insomnia refers to the inability to fall asleep or to remain asleep. It can be caused by jet lag, stress and anxiety, hormones, or digestive problems. It may also be a symptom of another condition.

Therapies for Sleep Deficiency: Over-the-counter drugs, music therapy, lavender pillow spray, and hydrotherapy (a soak in a hot bathtub within an hour of going to bed is a great way to relax) are some options.

Adjusting your daily schedule and activities may also prove beneficial. This includes avoiding caffeine and exercise near bedtime.

According to Healthline.com, essential oil blends are designed to promote sleep. These blends often incorporate oils such as lavender and chamomile, which have relaxing properties.

• **Allergies** - Allergies are an immune response triggered by allergens. Many allergens are everyday substances that are harmless to most people.

People with allergies have especially sensitive immune systems that react when they contact allergens. Common allergens include foods (nuts, eggs, milk, soy, shellfish, wheat), pollen, mold, latex, and pet dander.

Therapies for Allergies: The easiest and most effective way to treat allergies is to get rid of or avoid the cause. For example, with pollen allergies, avoid being outside when pollen counts are high and keep the windows to your room shut.

Because it is very difficult to avoid certain allergens, medication may be necessary to lessen symptoms caused by allergens, other than food and drugs.

• **Headaches** - Everyone suffers the occasional mild headache, but if you experience abnormally frequent headaches, you probably want to find relief. There are countless causes of headaches, which differ for each person, so you'll have to do some experimenting to figure out the cause of your pain. Some of the many causes of headaches include:

- Emotional stress
- Physical stress
- Irregular sleep habits (sleeping too much or too little)

Therapies for Headaches: According to the Mayo Clinic, hot packs and heating pads can relax tense muscles. Warm showers or baths may have a similar effect. In small amounts, caffeine alone can relieve migraine pain in the early stages or enhance the pain-reducing effects of acetaminophen (commonly through Tylenol and aspirin.) A headache can be a symptom of a serious condition, such as a stroke, meningitis, or encephalitis. See a doctor if you experience headaches that are more severe than usual.

• **Depression** - Mental and emotional pain can be as painful as physical pain. Depression can strike in mild or severe form and requires treatment of the whole body.

It is very important to make a distinction between situational depression, which is a normal reaction to events around us, and clinical (also called endogenous) depression, which is triggered from within and is not related to external situations. Situational depression is quite common and normally follows stressful situations or losses. Rather than suppress these feelings, it is best to work through these periods with help from psychologists or counselors. Clinical depression is a medical diagnosis and often requires other forms of depression treatment.

In Buddhist philosophy, depression represents the inevitable consequence of seeking stimulation. The centuries old teachings suggest that we seek balance in our emotional health and lives, rather than continuously striving for the highs, and then complaining about the lows that follow.

Therapies for Depression: Reduced levels of the following have been found in people with depression: magnesium, vitamin B2, B6, B12, folic acid and thyroid hormone. Ask your doctor to run some tests.

The ability to go to the calm quiet place within you is an asset in dealing with depression.

Its basic recommendation by Dr. Weil, encourages the daily practice of meditation, and this is perhaps the best way to address the root of depression and change it. This requires long-term commitment, however, as meditation does not produce immediate results.

Top Common Chronic Diseases

Well, as you can see, I am trying to bring awareness about different conditions that all of us as family caregivers might face with, so let's understand the basics about them.

There is a difference between chronic disease and popular symptoms. Sometimes, the common cold, will just go away on its own. Chronic diseases are slower to develop, may progress over time, and may have any number of warning signs or no signs at all.

I did not know that six in ten adults in the U.S. have a chronic disease, according to the CDC. Did you know? And four in ten adults in the U.S. have two or more diseases. We know that most chronic diseases can be prevented by eating well, being physically active, avoiding tobacco and excessive alcohol, and getting regular health screenings. CDC's National Center for Chronic Disease Prevention and Health Promotion (NCCDPHP) helps people and communities prevent chronic diseases and promotes health and wellness for all.

Healthy choices can reduce your likelihood of getting a chronic disease and improve your quality of life. Chronic diseases are something that doctors, and patients have struggled against for years. Age, family genetics, and gender make it nearly impossible for older adults to avoid becoming a chronic disease statistic.

Despite how common they are, many chronic diseases go undiagnosed and untreated for an extended period of time. The cause for that can be blamed on a lack of education and knowledge about the disease itself, and warning signs to look out for. Take a look at the 7 most common chronic diseases in the U.S. so you know what you may be at risk for!

Seven Common Chronic Diseases
- Dementia and Alzheimer's disease
- Diabetes
- Arthritis
- Heart failure
- Chronic kidney disease (CKD)
- Hypertension (high blood pressure)
- Inflammation

Let's review the fundamental of each chronic diseases in this next section:

• **Dementia** – Dementia is a collection of symptoms including memory loss, personality change, and impaired intellectual functions that result from disease or trauma to the brain. These changes are not part of normal aging and are severe enough to impact daily living, independence, and relationships. While Alzheimer's disease is the most common type of dementia, there are also many other forms, including vascular and mixed dementia.

Preventing dementia or delaying symptoms – Recent research suggests that healthy lifestyle habits and mental stimulation may help prevent dementia altogether. Just as physical exercise keeps you physically fit, exercising your mind and memory can help you stay mentally sharp, no matter the family history or age.

• **Diabetes** – Diabetes is a disease that occurs when your body is resistant to or doesn't produce enough insulin. Insulin is what your body uses to get energy from food and distribute it to your cells. When this doesn't happen, you get high blood sugar, which can lead to complications such as kidney disease, heart disease, or blindness. Chances of having diabetes increase after age 45.

According to the NIH (Dec. 2020), an estimated 30.3 million people in the United States, or 9.4% of the population, have diabetes. About one in four people with diabetes don't know they have the disease. An estimated 84.1 million Americans aged 18 years or older have prediabetes.

• **Arthritis** – Arthritis literally means joint inflammation. Although joint inflammation is a symptom or sign rather than a specific diagnosis, the term arthritis is often used to refer to any disorder that affects the joints. Joints are places where two bones meet, such as your elbow or knee.

According to the NIH, about 91 million U.S. adults may have some form of arthritis. This estimate is 68% higher than the previously reported estimate for arthritis—a term that includes multiple conditions that affect the joints, tissues around the joints, and other connective tissues.

• **Heart Failure** - Heart failure is a serious but common condition. In heart failure, the heart cannot pump enough blood to meet the body's needs. Heart failure develops over time as the pumping action of the heart gets weaker, or if it gets more difficult to adequately fill the heart with blood between heartbeats. It can affect either the right, the left, or both sides of the heart. Heart failure does not mean that the heart has stopped working or is about to stop working. According to the CDC, about 6.2 million adults in the United States have heart failure.

• **Chronic Kidney Disease (CKD)** - The kidneys are bean-shaped organs, each about the size of a fist, located near the middle of the back, just below the rib cage. Every day, the kidneys process about 200 quarts of blood to sift out about two quarts of metabolic wastes. The substances the kidneys remove includes the breakdown products of harmful compounds that get into our bodies one way or another. The waste and extra water become urine.

CKD is a condition in which the kidneys are damaged and cannot filter blood as well as they should. Because of this, excess fluid and waste from blood remain in the body and may cause other health problems, such as heart disease and stroke.

According to the CDC, more than one in seven, that is 15% of U.S. adults or 37 million people, are estimated to have CKD. As many as nine in ten adults with CKD do not know they have CKD. About two in five adults with severe CKD do not know they have CKD.

• **Hypertension (High Blood Pressure)** - Blood pressure is determined both by the amount of blood your heart pumps and the amount of resistance to blood flow in your arteries. The more blood your heart pumps and the narrower your arteries, the higher your blood pressure. According to the CDC, nearly half of adults in the United States (108 million, or 45%) have hypertension and are taking medication for it. Only about 1 in 4 adults (24%) with hypertension have their condition under control.

• **Inflammation** - If you have ever had a cold, a cut, a rash, or a bruise, then you have experienced inflammation.

Inflammation, which is a growing problem worldwide, can be caused by such things as poor nutrition, environmental toxins, genetics, reliance on medication, stress, and limited physical activity. However, when educated and prepared, you can take control of your health, both preventing inflammation from happening or managing it when it occurs.

There are some foods that are powerful in helping with inflammation. I've listed them below:

- **Leafy Greens**: Rich in vitamin K and offering powerful anti-inflammatory and anti-cancer effects, greens such as kale, collards, Bok-choy, and broccoli should be mainstays of your diet.
- **Berries**: All varieties are healthful.
- **Salmon and Black Cod**: Salmon is excellent as well as black cod, which has even more inflammation taming omega-3 fatty acids.
- **Ginger**: Along with having potent anti-inflammatory action, this root helps reduce intestinal gas and nausea.

Now, I am going to share another important matter in this next section: hormones.

Hormones

Another very important element in our body is hormones. Hormones are chemical messengers that are secreted directly into the blood, which carries them to organs and tissues of the body to exert their functions. There are many types of hormones that act on different aspects of bodily functions and processes.

The human body secretes and circulates some 50 different hormones. Some important hormones of the human body include the following: thyroid, insulin, estrogen, progesterone, testosterone, serotonin, and cortisol.

We need to keep our hormones in balance, but how? The more I studied about a healthy life, I found out that in every aspect of it, balancing our hormones naturally can be simple and so easy in most cases.

Easy Natural Ways to Balance Your Hormones

- **Eat Enough Protein** at every meal. According to Healthline.com, to optimize hormone health, experts recommend consuming a minimum of 20–30 grams of protein per meal.

- **Engage in Regular Exercise**. The CDC and HHS recommends 30 minutes daily of physical activity and twice weekly strength training exercises.

- **Avoid Sugar and Refined Carbs**. Carbohydrates aren't all bad, but some may be healthier than others. Choose your carbohydrates wisely. Limit foods with added sugars and refined grains, such as sugary drinks, desserts, and candy, which are packed with calories but low in nutrition. Instead, go for fruits, vegetables, and whole grains.

- **Learn to Manage Stress**. Stress can disrupt your body's natural hormone balance, causing issues such as obesity, insomnia, and low energy.

- **Consume Healthy Fats**, such as fatty fish. Eating healthy fats releases hormones, making the body feel full and reducing the odds of developing insulin resistance.

- **Avoid Overeating**. Stop overeating the foods that cause insulin resistance. Eat at least three meals per day, focusing on portion size, not calories, and including protein with each meal and snack.
- **Drink Green Tea**. According to Healthline.com, since green tea has other health benefits and most studies suggest that it may provide some improvement in insulin response, you may want to consider drinking one to three cups per day.

It could be easy to take care of our physical body by sleeping well, drinking water, exercise, manage stress, and consume healthy food. Our health matters more now as a caregiver. We have a loved one who is depending on us.

To keep it simple, focus on the four most important hormones to help us family caregivers to stay happier: endorphins (reduce feeling of pain), serotonin (mood stabilizer), dopamine (pleasure), oxytocin (love and trust).

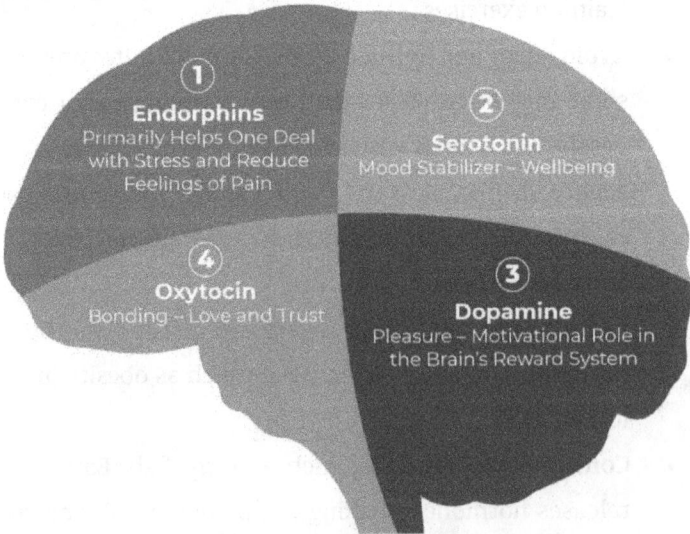

Image 7-1 Happy Hormones

BONUS CHAPTER – PRACTICING YOUR NEW HEALTHY LIFESTYLE

THIS CHAPTER PROVIDES YOU some extra bonuses and exercises available only in this book to keep you healthier and happier.

- Bonus #1 - Who doesn't want to feel younger, to have sharper brain, and more energy?
- Bonus #2 – Access to quick natural remedies
- Bonus #3 – Activities for a healthier lifestyle
- Bonus #4 – Chart of the best fruits and vegetables
- Bonus #5 – Cooking recipes for breakfast, lunch, and dinner. Recipes only available in this book!
- Bonus #6 – Fun with puzzles
- Bonus #7 – Weekly journal

Bonus #1: Feel and Look Younger

Every day I ask myself, *"how can I make a better day?"*

I make a list of my interests, hobbies, and activities. I refer to my list every day to see if there is something I would like to pursue to make my day more uplifting.

There are many things you can do such as learn a new language, solve a puzzle, learn a new recipe, and/or instrument. Make sure to spend time with friends and family. Share your healthy journey with them.

Traveling is another way to feel young. You do not have to travel long distance. You can travel to your local museum or even town center.

Take care of your skin daily by gently cleansing. I like to use rosewater. Rosewater can be used as a toner and cleanser on all skin types. After washing your face with a mild face wash, apply 1 tablespoon of rosewater on your face.

Next apply a moisturizer, allowing your skin to stay firm and elastic. Reducing the appearance of wrinkles. Look for moisturizers with ingredients such as green tea extract, vitamins A, C & E, and hyaluronic, which will increase collagen and retains moisture.

Celebrate yourself by taking a spa day for yourself. Get a massage, sign up for a makeover, or buy a new outfit. Anything that brings a smile to your face will boost your spirit and renew your inner glow.

Most importantly, take it easy. Stressing less means staying young. Every day for about 15 minutes, relax, and meditate, or just breathe deeply, while letting worries melt away and helping yourself look younger, naturally.

Bonus #2: Quick Natural Remedies

According to WebMD, no matter what you've heard or how badly you want relief, talk with your doctor or pharmacist before trying any home remedy. This is even more important if you take prescription or over-the-counter medications because some can affect how drugs work. And keep in mind that many don't have any research to back them up. Following, I provide home remedies:

Peppermint. Peppermint mint has been used for hundreds of years as a health remedy. Peppermint oil might help with irritable bowel syndrome—a long-term condition that can cause cramps, bloating, gas, diarrhea, and constipation—and it may be good for headaches as well.

Honey. This natural sweetener may work just as well for a cough as over-the-counter medicines. It is a natural antibiotic.

Turmeric. This spice has been hyped as being able to help with a variety of conditions from arthritis to fatty liver. There is some early research to support this. Other claims, such as healing ulcers and helping with skin rashes after radiation are lacking proof. If you try it, don't overdo it. High doses can cause digestive problems.

Ginger. It's been used for thousands of years in Asian medicine to treat stomach aches, diarrhea, nausea, and vomiting. But some people get tummy trouble, so, talk to your doctor, and use it with care.

Green Tea. This comforting drink does more than keep you awake and alert. It's a great source of some powerful antioxidants that can protect your cells from damage and help you fight disease.

Garlic. Some studies show that people who eat more garlic are less likely to get certain types of cancer (garlic supplements doesn't seem to have the same effect). It may also lower blood cholesterol and blood pressure levels.

Cardamom. Some of the health benefit of cardamom is protecting from chronic disease because it has anti-inflammatory effect. It may treat bad breath and prevent cavities.

Bonus #3: Activities for a Healthier Lifestyle

There are 3 core activities that can impact your life to remain healthy.

- **Laughing.** It's no secret that laughing feels good. But did you know it can provide stress relief and other health benefits?

  We change physiologically when we laugh. Laughter shuts down the release of stress hormones like cortisol. It also triggers the production of feel-good neurochemicals—such as dopamine—which have calming, anti-anxiety benefits. Here are some possible health benefits of laughter:
    - Soothes tension
    - Relieves pain (endorphin hormone)
    - Connect with people (dopamine and oxytocin hormones)
    - Improves your mood (serotonin hormone)
    - Burns calories

- **Gardening.** Yes, gardening again! Roll up your sleeves and get digging, planting, and weeding this spring and summer. Here's how tending to your garden beds will benefit you in the long run: gardening burns a lot of calories, it can lower your blood pressure, spending time outside prompts your body to make vitamin D, gardening can relieve stress, and gardening can make you happier.

- **Watching Good Movies.** Watching movies can help us make sense of our own lives. For thousands of years, knowledge and wisdom have been passed down through the art of storytelling. Stories offer us different perspectives and help us understand and make sense of the world. And movies are stories. Here are my favorite list of movies that keeps me happy: Something's Gotta Give (2003), My Fair Lady (1964), La La Land (2016), Mamma Mia! (2008), Groundhog Day (1993), The Sound of Music (1965), My Big Fat Greek Wedding (2002)

Bonus #4: Chart for Best Fruits and Vegetables

The chart below is info I've gathered from different accredited organizations. Below are health benefits of some fruits and vegetables.

Fruits and Vegetables	Health Benefits	Resources
Apple	**Lung Health** because flavonoids in apple skin reduce inflammation and strength tissues. Reduces risk of pneumonia.	Finnish Researchers
Pear	**Loss weight**, a half of a pear each morning causes you to loss 12 pound a year, because of fiber and how pears affect the hypothalamus in brain that controls hunger	Penn State Scientists
Persimmon	**Helps with stress and you'll be calmer** in 12 minutes because of tannic and gallic acids that stimulate the brain's limbic system.	British scientists
Plum	One or two plums at a meal eases tiredness for up to 3 hours, because it activates genes that heighten insulin sensitivity and blood glucose control.	UCLA scientists
Pomegranate Seeds	**Blood pressure:** 1/2 cup daily for four weeks will reduce the blood pressure.	Journal National Science
Pumpkin	**Ache Stopper:** 2½ cups of pumpkin end the ache because of anti-inflammatories in pumpkin.	USDA Researcher
Spinach	**Calm anxiety:** 1 cup a day stop edginess and tension could plunge by 50% in as little as three days, because of carotenoids that producing amygdala in the brain.	UCLA Researchers
Sweet Potatoes	**Calms muscle tension:** 1 cup a day then brings 33% calmer and happier in five days, because of manganese, copper, and beta-carotene that soothe the central nervous system.	Australian investigators
Tomatoes	**Anti-Aging:** 4 cups weekly can erase dryness and fine lines. So, 5 years younger looking in just one month, because Vitamin C and flavonoids switch on enzymes that repair aging skin cells.	The National Center for Biotechnology Information (NCBI)

Bonus #5: Cooking Recipes for Breakfast, Lunch, and Dinner (Serving for 1)

- **Breakfast Option #1: Pita, Feta Cheese, Honey, and Tea**

This is my favorite breakfast; it is a Persian tradition used every single day!

Small whole wheat Pita Bread (70 calories) with feta cheese (1 cube serving is 70 calories.)

Greek feta cheese is made from sheep or goat milk, and because of it has lower calories than any other cheese, it is healthier choice, but remember that it is high in sodium, so it is better to rinse the cheese before you have it. But do not rinse too much that it takes away the flavor.

Black tea has approximately 2 calories per cup. Adding 1 teaspoon of honey to your bread or tea contains 21 calories.

This breakfast totals 163 Calories.... Delicious with little calories.

- **Breakfast Option #2: One Soft Boiled Egg, Whole Wheat Toast, Cup of Coffee or Black Tea, Plus Banana.**

This one is an easy and classy breakfast.

One large, boiled egg contains about 78 calories. It is high in nutrients.

Whole-wheat bread, 1 medium slice, is about 70 Calories.

While plain brewed coffee contains almost no calories, coffee with dairy products, sugar, and other flavorings is much higher in calories.

Without milk and sugar so far you have 148 calories, not bad. But if you add one small banana which has about 100 calories, your total calories will jump to 248, still is not bad at all.

- **Lunch Option #1: Tuna Sandwich**

Canned tuna is a good source of essential nutrients, such as omega-3 fatty acids, high-quality protein. This easy and delicious lunch can be made using two slices of whole-wheat bread, 3 ounces of water-packed tuna and 1 tablespoon of light mayo. You'll create a sandwich of about 310 calories.

You can add these additional items:

- I mix one chopped leaf celery. It is healthy and a low-calorie addition that gives your lunch an extra crunch. It has about 7 calories.
- 1 slice of tomato (1 thin/small slice) contains 18 calories.
- There are 4 calories in 1 leaf outer of green leaf lettuce.

You have a total of 340 calories and a great healthy lunch.

My daughter and I cut this sandwich in half. Then we each add a half of a medium apple and sometimes a slick of pickle to our sandwich.

There are 36 calories in a 1/2 medium apple.

There are 3 calories in 1 slice (0.7 oz) pickled kosher dill sandwich slices.

So, my typical lunch sandwich, if I take both the slick of pickle and half an apple has just about a total of 212 calories.

Do NOT forget your glass of water!

- **Lunch Option #2: Power Wrap (Vegetable Wrap)**

Spread avocado on the whole wheat tortilla. Add veggies of your choice and roll it up. Cut it in half before serving. If you can share it with someone great. Otherwise, put the other half in refrigerator for the next day.

Then you can add fat free Greek yogurt to your lunch.

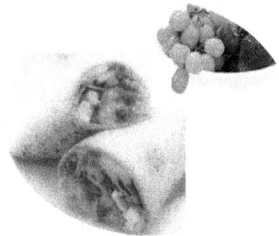

One 10-inch whole wheat tortilla contains 110 calories.

Light mayo per tablespoon contains 45 calories.

There are 24 calories in 1 cup of raw vegetable.

Half an avocado contains around 160 calories.

I like spicy foods; so, adding half a cup of jalapeno contains 13 calories.

Total of 352 calories.

So, cutting that sandwich in half means only 176 calories. Then we could add 1 cup red seedless grapes for 100 calories or cup of strawberries for 49 calories.

Then the total of calories is under 300. Not bad at all.

- **Dinner Option #1: Salmon**

Salmon is known as the number one healthy food for supporting all your organs. Salmon is rich in omega-3 fatty acids that can help reduce inflammation, lower blood pressure, and decrease risk factors for diseases. It's a great source of protein, potassium, and selenium, a mineral that protects bone health, improves thyroid function, and reduces the risk of cancer. Salmon can also help reduce the risk of heart disease, aid in weight control, and protect brain health.

No matter how you want to cook it, in the oven, grill, stove, or bake it, it still is your best dinner option. And if you use the right ingredient (just a little) you will have a delicious dinner most of the nights.

There are 158 calories in 4 ounces of cooked salmon which is considered a healthy serving size. I like to add salt and pepper and garlic. Salmon only needs about 2 minutes on the stovetop and 5-7 minutes in the oven with the same ingredients (salt and pepper) and a touch of olive oil and a zest of 1 large lemon. Do not have it turn brown. In the oven put it in a piece of foil and add layers of lemon slices on top of the salmon.

For a side dish, have green beans. There are 44 calories in 1 cup of fresh cooked green string beans. The total of calories for your dinner is only 202.

• **Dinner Option #2: Vegetable Soup**

This vegetable soup is healthy, it's comforting, and a thousand times better than what you'll get in a can! Full of flavor and so easy to make you can't go wrong with a big, warm bowl of vegetable soup.

You can put whatever vegetables you like in this soup, from seasonal fresh veggies to frozen. Here's a sample list to get you going: Carrots, celery, tomatoes, green beans, corn, yellow onion, and garlic. 2 tablespoon of olive oil, 1 1/2 cups chopped yellow onion, 2 cups peeled and chopped carrots, 1 1/4 cups chopped celery, 4 cloves garlic, minced, 4 (14.5 oz) cans low sodium chicken broth or vegetable broth, 2 (14.5 oz) cans diced tomatoes (undrained), 1/3 cup chopped fresh parsley, 2 bay leaves, 1/2 teaspoon dried thyme, salt and freshly ground black pepper, 1 1/2 cups chopped frozen or fresh green beans, 1 1/4 cups frozen or fresh corn.

Instructions:

Heat olive oil in a large pot over medium-high heat.

Add onions, carrots, and celery and sauté for 4 minutes then add garlic and sauté 30 seconds longer.

Add in broth tomatoes, parsley, bay leaves, thyme, and season with salt and pepper to taste.

Bring to a boil, then add green beans.

Add corn and cook 5 minutes longer. Serve warm.

• **Dessert Option: Select Your Fresh Fruit**

Have Fun Creating and Naming Your Own Recipes

Create your own recipes and name them.

When my son was about 5 years old, he and I decided to make a lunch together with green beans onion and eggs dish. We loved it and we named it "KavEli" combination of the first 3 letters of our names.

I think this is the way we could enjoy and share our creation together with others.

- **CucuYogu (Combining Cucumber and Yogurt)**

For example, one of my favorite side dishes that could be great for snack time is Greek yogurt and cubed cucumber, but you can make it the way you want it. I like it with dill weed, minced clove garlic and any herbs that I can pick that day from my garden, and sometimes I add raisin to it too.

I am listing some ingredient for your next refreshing cucumber and yogurt snack.

I named it CucuYogu. My recipe is below, but you can add based on what you have available that day and make it your own. Of course, name it as well.

- 1 (32 ounce) container plain yogurt
- 2 cucumbers, peeled and cubed
- 1 clove garlic, minced (optional)
- 4 tablespoons dried dill weed or (2 tablespoons any combination of finely chopped fresh parsley, cilantro, basil, and tarragon). I use what I grow in my backyard.
- 1 teaspoon ground or crumbled dried rose petals (optional)
- 2 tablespoons roughly chopped toasted walnut pieces (optional)
- 1 teaspoon salt
- 1 teaspoon pepper

- **FePi (Combining Feta Cheese and Pita Bread)**

With pita bread and feta cheese, you can make your own taco. If you add a touch of honey, you are making great breakfast. However, instead of honey if you add a slice of tomato that becomes lunch. This is the snack I like to have at the pool side in the summer.

Another option is you can have pita bread and feta cheese with a bunch of grapes and a glass of wine as your light dinner. I like to add some chopped cilantro and sometimes chopped walnut for more of a flavor. You can rename it to your own recipe.

One more option you can make with pita bread and feta cheese is adding sliced boiled eggs. Again, you can add chopped parsley or cilantro.

Bonus item. One ingredient that goes well with pita bread and feta cheese is olives. Try it and see how you like it.

- **TATA (Combining Pasta and Feta Cheese)**

I do not know why I call it TATA, but perhaps because it is so good for many things that you can make with it. The convenience of this dish is that I can make it the night before and have it for lunch or as my side dish at dinner.

I like to make it with whole wheat pasta and any vegetable that I can find in my refrigerator like zucchini, cucumber, tomato, and/or celery. It is healthier if you add some fresh herbs to it. If you add fresh chopped parsley or cilantro that makes this dish so yummy.

For protein, I add cubed feta cheese and cooked black beans. You can add sliced olives. Add one tablespoon olive oil and vinegar plus touch of salt and pepper as its dressing. If you like, this is optional, you can add 2 tablespoon of lemon juice.

I try to keep a small bowl of cooked whole wheat or whole grain pasta in different shapes (ex: bowties) in the refrigerator so it is ready to go when needed.

Note if refrigerating: make sure you add 3-4 tablespoons of olive oil before you frigid the bowl to keep it fluffy. Do not add feta until you want to serve it.

- **ZAZAZA (Flatbread Pizza)**

Another favorite dish of mine is the flatbread pizza. Most grocery stores sell pre-made flatbreads, which will work well with this recipe.

When you have the flatbread, all you'll need to choose is your favorite pizza toppings such as combining tomato, fresh mozzarella, basil, olive oil, and a little oregano.

Heat the oven to 400 degrees. Line a baking sheet large enough to fit two flatbreads.

- 2 flatbreads
- 2 tablespoon extra-virgin olive oil
- 5 ounces sliced fresh mozzarella cheese
- 8 fresh basil leaves
- 12 cherry tomatoes, thinly sliced
- 1 teaspoon salt and fresh ground black pepper
- 1 tablespoon dried oregano

Brush the olive oil over the bread. Layer the sliced mozzarella, basil leaves, and the sliced tomatoes on top. Season the flatbread with salt, fresh ground pepper, and the oregano. Bake the pizza for 10 to 15 minutes.

Add a little extra of olive oil and some more chopped fresh basil leaves before your serve. Enjoy and ZAZAZA it.

Bonus # 6: Three (3) Puzzles

Always find time for solving some puzzles. You can buy a booklet for a different kind of puzzle or go to your computer and find thousands of free puzzles. Try something new, not too hard, but choose one that challenges you. Can you do the next three puzzles that I have made for you?

- **Puzzle # 1 (Vitamin / Nutrient Food Pairings)**

Match perfect food pairings for the following vitamins / nutrients. Review the chapter about vitamins and minerals to find the right match. The answers are at the end of this chapter.

Vitamin D	
Vitamin B12	
Vitamin E	
Vitamin C	
Vitamin K	

- **Puzzle #2 (Crossword Puzzle)**

I'm positively challenging you to solve this puzzle. The answers are at the end of this chapter.

	10-								
			2-		6-				
		3-		7-					
5-	1-		4-						
						9-			
			8-						

Down
1- I am Fruit, not vegetable, source of Vitamin C, E, K, B6, and Omega-3
4- With or without partner I improve your heart, and your mental and strength your bones.
7- I filter the blood, I am organ, and I like Green tea, Garlic, Grapes, and Grapefruit.
9- I am largest organ in your body.

Row
2- This Vegetable contains many Vitamins and minerals, specially vitamin C, Iron, magnesium, potassium.
3- Best dinner ever, offers Omega-3 which helps heart and bones.
5- This activity exposure you to Vitamin D, decrease dementia and benefit you bones.
6- I protect you against diseases, you born with me.
8- Vitamin D and I could protect you against many diseases. Your body needs me to build strong bones.
10- I am smallest but worse enemy of your health

- **Puzzle #3 (Word Search)**

Can you find these 7 body words in the following puzzle?

- Skeletal
- Muscular
- Cardiovascular
- Digestive
- Endocrine
- Nervous
- Respiratory

A	C	K	X	Y	Z	A	B	D	L	M	T	I	O	P
L	V	A	F	W	A	P	J	M	T	D	L	B	F	A
E	C	Y	R	Q	X	Y	O	Z	V	Y	A	A	G	L
W	B	E	N	D	O	C	R	I	N	E	D	Q	H	V
M	U	K	P	I	I	E	P	B	U	Y	R	P	C	N
V	I	R	L	G	P	O	W	E	E	B	A	O	S	D
I	E	T	M	E	J	Y	V	N	C	V	L	W	J	T
O	L	Y	G	S	G	P	D	A	T	N	U	A	P	S
P	P	L	A	T	E	L	E	K	S	S	C	N	A	P
D	T	I	T	I	T	N	W	W	Z	C	S	Y	N	K
T	S	U	O	V	R	E	N	U	Q	X	U	T	E	C
B	B	O	F	E	O	Q	Z	I	W	I	M	L	W	M
K	P	P	R	O	B	Z	P	O	E	P	G	R	A	H
X	A	W	D	Y	R	O	T	A	R	I	P	S	E	R

Bonus # 7: Weekly Journal

In the following pages, I have provided a week journal to get you going on creating a mindful habit to your healthy journey. Make copies of these pages for your on-going weeks.

Date: ___ / ___ / ___ Week #	Write down your thoughts
What did you learn today?	
What activity did you do today?	
What did you do to relax today?	
Date: ___ / ___ / ___	Write down your thoughts
What did you learn today?	
What activity did you do today?	
What did you do to relax today?	
Date: ___ / ___ / ___	Write down your thoughts
What did you learn today?	
What activity did you do today?	
What did you do to relax today?	
Date: ___ / ___ / ___	Write down your thoughts
What did you learn today?	
What activity did you do today?	
What did you do to relax today?	
Date: ___ / ___ / ___	Write down your thoughts
What did you learn today?	
What activity did you do today?	
What did you do to relax today?	
Date: ___ / ___ / ___	Write down your thoughts
What did you learn today?	
What activity did you do today?	
What did you do to relax today?	
Date: ___ / ___ / ___	Write down your thoughts
What did you learn today?	
What activity did you do today?	
What did you do to relax today?	

Answers for Puzzle # 1

Vitamin D	In addition to pairing vitamin D with calcium, avocados, nuts, seeds, full-fat dairy Products, and eggs are nutritious sources of fat that help boost your vitamin D absorption. Studies indicate that having vitamin D with a large meal or source of fat can significantly increase absorption. Magnesium assists in the activation of vitamin D.
Vitamin B12	B12 absorption can be increased by taking folate (another B vitamin, this one found in higher amounts in chickpeas, liver, pinto beans, lentils, spinach, asparagus, and avocado, among others).
Vitamin E	Foods that are rich in vitamin E include wheat germ oil, grains, nuts, seeds, green leafy vegetables, avocado, and dried prunes, while veggies, like broccoli, kale, spinach, cauliflower, cabbage, and Brussels sprouts are high in vitamin K.
Vitamin C	Vitamin C and Iron: a perfect match. Some doctors suggest taking a vitamin C supplement or drinking orange juice with your iron pill. This can help the iron absorb into your body.
Vitamin K	Excess amounts of vitamin E can reduce the absorption of vitamin K, while moderate amounts in combination—like spinach (vitamin K) and oil-based salad dressing (vitamin E)— shouldn't do much harm, but higher doses can be problematic.

Answers for Puzzle # 2

	10-B	A	C	T	E	R	I	A	
		2-S	P	6-I	N	A	C	H	
	3-S	A	7-L	M	O	N			
			I	M					
			V	U					
5-G	1-A	R	4-D	E	N	I	N	G	
	V		A	R	E		9-S		
	O		N				K		
	C		8-C	A	L	C	I	U	M
	A		I				N		
	D		N						
	O		G						

Resources

A healthy lifestyle is an ongoing journey, and you should keep searching for new information. Make sure your sources are accredited.

The growing popularity of the internet has made finding health information easier and faster. Much of the information on the internet is valuable; however, the internet also allows rapid and widespread distribution of false and misleading information. You should carefully consider the source of information you find on the internet and discuss that information with your health care provider. It is important to evaluate what you find on the internet because:

- Anyone can post information on the internet.
- Search engine results are selected by computer software and not by human experts.
- Websites may be sponsored by companies that are selling products so it may not provide objective information.

Here is a helpful list of resources for valid health information. Always remember that while there is a wealth of information online, much of it is not accurate, it is simply a fad, or trying to sell you something.

I Recommend the Following Websites:
- Centers for Disease Control & Prevention: www.cdc.gov/
- Mayo Clinic: www.mayoclinic.org/
- WebMD: www.webmd.com/
- National Institutes of Health: www.nih.gov/
- General nutrition information: www.nutrition.gov

My Favorite Health Magazines
- Prevention
- Psychology Today
- Life Extension
- Health
- Nutrition
- Alternative Medicine
- Experiencing Life

Books that Helped My Research
- Nutrition for Life, by Lisa Hark, RhD and Darwin Deen, MD.
- Every Heart Attack is Preventable, by Michael Moghadam, MD.
- Reversing Diabetes, by Neal D. Barnard, MD.
- The Vitamins & Minerals Bible
- Mind over Meds, by Andrew Weil, MD
- Natural Therapies, by Peter Albright, MD.
- The Anti-Inflammatory Diet & Action Plan, by Dorothy Calimeris and Sondi Bruner

Knowing your health history is important but sharing it with your doctor may be more important. That's because your doctor can help you interpret what it means for your current lifestyle, suggest prevention tips, and decide on screening or testing options for conditions you may be more at risk for.

Remember that every day there is some new discovery. As a family caregiver to another family caregiver, embrace this journey and continue your research for a healthier and happier life. Remember to self-love to be able to effectively self-care!

I hope after you read this book you keep researching and visit my website and connect for more findings at, www.myserenity.love

www.ingramcontent.com/pod-product-compliance
Lightning Source LLC
Chambersburg PA
CBHW062004040426
42447CB00010B/1903